How to Treat your Employees Like a Dog

How to Treat your Employees Like a Dog

Russell J. Hornfisher

Izell Leadership

www.izellleadership.com

First edition

First printing 2018

ISBN 978-0-9998618-0-6

Dedication

The person most responsible for this book is Bonnie, my wife. She introduced me to the fascinating world of dogs. Far more important, for over half of my time on earth, she has been my partner in the journey we call life. She is the Yin to my Yang pulling me back into focus when I become obtuse. Most important, she is the love of my life

Acknowledgements

Any significant accomplishment in life is the result of many individual contributions, which is definitely the case with this book. I would like to express my deepest appreciation to the friends who helped me complete the endeavor.

The readers and editors applied their unique backgrounds. Their experiences include teachers, psychology, journalism, and business professionals. Many are dog trainers and exhibitors, all are dog lovers. These friends organized my ramblings, fine-tuned, massaged, corrected, and polished my words. They are Lisa Allmendinger, James Biga, Shelley Devereaux, Brian Gustin, Dr. Joanne Kanas, Joy Knapp, Walter O'Brien, Dr. Melodie Sorenson, Marilyn Tomaszewski, and Jozef Venner.

My vision would not be complete without artistic talent provided by creative artist, Kim Hunley, who captured each dog's personality, bringing life to my words and graphic artist, Eva Wawrowski, whose creative cover design energized the title and the book.

Table on Contents

Today, you are the culmination

of all decisions you have made

and people you have met to this

point in your life.

No one else has had the same

experience or personal

relationships you have had.

**Your behavior towards others, trains
them how to treat you in the future.**

Chapter One

BONNIE

During the 1980's while working as a pharmaceutical sales rep, I spent my evenings attending Eastern Michigan University in pursuit of a Master's Degree in Organizational Behavior and Development (MSOD). Since my real job was full-time, 40+ hours per week, I was limited in the number of hours per week and time of day I could spend attending classes, which meant attending night classes.

Working on a Master's Degree as a part-time student took six years to complete. My thesis alone took nearly two years. When I first started taking evening classes at EMU, the goal was an MBA. But during my third year of attending evening classes at EMU my curriculum called for a class titled Organizational Development. This was a class on motivation and reward systems which caused me to change my directions and pursue a Master of Science in Organization Behavior and Development (MSOD) degree.

Classes in MSOD taught me important things such as Maslow's Hierarchy of needs, operant conditioning, social learning theory, and many other principles used to explain why people do the things they do and how to direct their behavior. The independent research that I conducted for my Master's thesis further stimulated my interest into why people do the things they do, and how to get them to do the things I want them to do. The years of study and classes taken were well spent, learning how to get people to work harder, take on more challenging tasks, and learn new jobs.

While working on my MSOD degree, I met a woman who would change my life. Bonnie was, and still is, the love of my life. She has had a powerful impact on my life in many ways. To start with she is a very interesting individual. Her Bachelor's Degree is in pharmacy from The University of Michigan, but after graduation and working as a hospital pharmacist, for two years, she realized Pharmacy was not her calling in life. So, she looked for another career that was more to her interests by becoming a pharmaceutical sales representative.

This was the job she had at the time we met. In addition to working full time as a pharmaceutical sales rep, she was working on a master's degree at Wayne State University. Similar to me, she was a part-time student at night, pursuing a Master's Degree in Business Administration (MBA), with an emphasis in accounting.

Our daily routines were very similar, work by day, school in the evenings, except she had the added responsibility of a high energy, crazy, male, golden retriever named Sonny. Bonnie made her priorities in life very simple – Sonny, the golden retriever, was her top priority. If anyone wanted to get involved in her life, then it was going to involve Sonny. So, I began spending more time with this big goofy dog. Sonny was fun, very smart, and it wasn't long before the three of us were married. Though we were married, it wasn't until I gave Bonnie an 8-week-old golden retriever puppy for Valentine's Day, that it solidified in her mind my commitment to the concept – love me, love my dog, which now became plural dogs.

Golden retriever puppies can be destructive, but Bonnie was very skilled at teaching household manners, which made our dogs easy to live with. Bonnie had been training and showing dogs in obedience competition since she was eleven years old, she had a passion for training and showing dogs, and she was very good at teaching dogs how to behave. As excellent as Bonnie was at training dogs, I did not understand anything about what she was doing, nor did I care. As long as the dogs behaved themselves that worked great for me.

After receiving her MBA, and passing the examination to become a certified public accountant, Bonnie accepted a job with a small local accounting firm. For her, the work environment and hours seemed like the perfect job. She spent her days at work as a CPA thus leaving her evenings to be at home teaching our dogs good household manners.

After a little more than a year working in an accounting firm, Bonnie was beginning to realize her job, as a CPA, wasn't much different than what she experienced as a pharmacist.
Shortly after I had finished my Master's Degree, a job opportunity in sales management provided us a chance to move to Denver, Colorado. This gave Bonnie a good reason to quit her job working for a small local CPA firm. When we moved to Denver, Bonnie quickly found a job with, what then was, one of the, Big Eight accounting firms, in a high rise office building downtown Denver. To Bonnie, how could anything get better than working as a CPA for an international accounting firm?

But after about a year, Bonnie realized working as a CPA – whether it was for a small local CPA firm or a large international company – wasn't as great as she had expected. This was neither her dream job, nor was it anything she wanted to do long term. She

17

discovered working for a CPA firm wasn't much different than working as a pharmacist. Bonnie did not enjoy working as either a pharmacist or an accountant. She spent eight hours a day, five days per week wishing for the weekend. Wishing your life away is no way to live.

Life is especially miserable if you hate getting up every morning to do a job you don't enjoy. So, it was time for her third career change, which is where the story gets entertaining.

After numerous evening conversations about what she wanted to do career-wise, Bonnie was consistent with what she wanted – her number one priority was her dogs; she wanted a job where she could take her dogs to work. We searched long and hard through the classified ads and job listings, but were not successful finding anything that stated:

"Pharmacist wanted, must have golden retriever."

Or

"CPA needed, job requires a dog."

So, we did the next most logical thing – we opened a pet supply store. Bonnie's accounting experience was very useful for writing a business plan with detailed financials. In addition, with our combined sales experience, we created a great marketing plan. But what we learned is lending institutions don't really care about great business ideas and plans, since over 70 percent of new retail startup business fail in the first five years. What they wanted was retail experience, a skill neither of us had. This limited our options, so we did the next most logical thing; we took money out of our savings and retirement programs to start a new retail pet supply store. (At this point, it's important to note we had no intentions of selling any live animals; our focus was strictly pet supplies.)

This venture was the beginning of our education in owning a retail business, and it's very tough work! But because Bonnie could take her dogs to work with her, she found it to be fun. Bonnie went from wearing business suits and heels to blue jeans and T-shirts; from sitting at a desk or working under a laminator flow hood to stacking bags of dog food. The woman was amazing!

She worked incredibly long hours and enjoyed every minute of it, especially her time with the dogs. Not only was Bonnie running a start-up business, but in a very short time she was involved in the local chamber of commerce and local small business associations.

Next she volunteered her time at Denver Children's Hospital involved in the creation of a program called "Prescription Pet" through which two dogs per day would visit patients. For a dog to visit a patient in the hospital, they first, needed a prescription from their physician. This was a structured program with specific end goals for each patient. It wasn't a program where dogs wandering around the halls of Children's Hospital hoping to get some attention. The participating patients had to have a specific reason for a dog to visit and activity that would benefit the patient's outcome.

Lesson No. 1: Follow your passion.

This is an important lesson I have repeatedly told, either as an adjunct instructor on the first meeting of University classes or teaching opportunities with co-workers. Bonnie worked very hard to obtain two college degrees preparing her for a very respectable career, and then passing licensure exams for each. But she wasn't doing what she loved. By following her passion and making a drastic career change, she went from dreading going to work every day, to bounding out of bed in the morning excited to get to work. Yes, such a change had tradeoffs. Bonnie switched careers discarding two jobs that offered prestige, good pay and status to run a start-up retail pet supply store. At this job, she worked long hours, seven days per week, with little to no pay, and had a lot of responsibility. But for her, the tradeoff was well worth it. She was being true to herself and had achieved her dream job, which involved taking her dogs to work with her.

If you pursue your passion, you will do a good job.
If you are good at your job, people will pursue you for your talent.

If you hate your job, it shows. If you are not happy, not having fun, just going through motions, doing a job to collect a paycheck, you will never excel. Nor will you ever reach your potential.

With the newly opened store beginning to grow, a friend who bred golden retrievers sent us a puppy. Bonnie was already overwhelmed by the number of things involved in running a new retail business. I was working long hours as a sales manager for a manufacturing company. With all of this responsibility, who had time to train a new puppy?

So, this new puppy arrived and as a golden retriever puppy will typically do, she chewed on anything and everything. Did I mention earlier Bonnie had always been responsible for all of our dogs' training! My involvement with the two previous Golden Retrievers, Sonny and Cindy, had always been the simple things, like cleaning up the yard waste, sometimes taking them for walks, or occasionally feeding them.

You get the idea; I was more kennel help than dog trainer.

By now, the new puppy had destroyed a variety of items in the house and needed training. Both Sonny and Cindy accompanied Bonnie everywhere; they were trained, and did whatever Bonnie told them to do. They really did not pay much attention to me; but they were very respectful of our house and belongings.

Bonnie had been training and showing dogs for decades and was good at it. But with all Bonnie was doing to build a new business, she did not have the time to train the little puppy.

Trust me, there is a point, this is where the story gets interesting.

I had a discussion with Bonnie one night about training the new puppy, we'd named Heidi. "Heidi needs to be trained," I told

Bonnie. "You are such a great dog trainer you can correct all of her destructive behaviors."

I thought I had a really good argument going. I was sure this would result in another well-behaved dog trained by Bonnie, the family trainer. But she wasn't responding exactly how I had expected. Somehow during the discussion, which I started, mind you, I thought by serving up a challenge, that was supposed to stimulate a reaction resulting in Bonnie training Heidi.

It didn't.

So I pushed further, thinking a threat might work. This is where I made a very bad tactical error, I said, "All right, if you don't train Heidi, I will," which in the heat of a discussion, I thought would further bait Bonnie into taking the challenge. Instead, it took a much unexpected U-turn. Somehow, I am not sure how, I ended up as the guy responsible for training the new puppy. (The art of negotiating, or lack thereof, is material for another book).

The next thing I knew, Bonnie registered **me** for a dog obedience seminar, which was an 8-hour, full day Saturday, program on dog obedience. During the first four hours, in the morning, a highly recognized, well accomplished dog trainer lectured participants on basic dog obedience techniques ... such as Maslow's Hierarchy of needs, operant conditioning, social learning theory, etc.(sounding familiar?) and other principles used to explain why dogs do the things they do, and how to direct their behavior. I spent six years working on a master's degree in business, at a highly respected University learning these theories and here they were in a dog obedience class?

The next four hours, in the afternoon, were spent actually working with our dogs, referred to as workshop, applying the theories taught in the morning session on our dogs. Although I completed the course, I do not believe I was the prized student. But I was hooked. These were the same principles I had spent six years learning in graduate school.

21

- How to motivate.
- How to create desired behavior.
- How to extinguish undesirable behavior.

But in a dog training class?

The theories and techniques presented at this dog training seminar were years ahead of the theories taught in graduate level management classes.

I had to learn more.

And thus began my quest for more dog training knowledge and education. Not only for the puppy at the end of my lead, but also for the many people I have interacted with in my business life.

I spent six years working on a Master's Degree in college; learning the same principles taught in an eight hours dog obedience class, though I say this in jest, it speaks volumes about the techniques used in training and motivating animals. They are way ahead of the skills and techniques used to train and manage people.

Since that most memorable day, at my first dog obedience seminar, I have found the books I most enjoy reading are about animal training. Because I take what I've learned from dog training and adapt these techniques to create applications for the management and motivation of people. I've found dogs to be little training laboratories. I can test training and motivation techniques on these willing subjects. When I find things which work, I then work on adapting these exercises for people.

It is important to understand that dog training is not about training a dog; it is about training a handler to train a dog. The skills and techniques learned in dog training can easily be applied to a parent raising a child, or training a manager to run a department or a building a marriage, or....

After getting a taste of success using behavioral motivation skills training dogs, I then look for way to transfer what I have learned to using these same skills on humans. I am constantly looking for opportunities and challenges where I can apply dog training to human leadership.

Bonnie had always purchased puppies from highly knowledgeable breeders. When you can start training with an 8-week-old puppy, it's like painting on a clean canvas – At such an early stage in life there aren't many, if any, bad habits. All training is a new experience for the puppy.

Since the puppy does not have entrenched behaviors or loyalties, training usually flows smoothly. With puppies, creating new behavior is direct and uncomplicated.

Several years after selling the pet supply store and moving to Iowa, Bonnie was asked by a local Humane Society to become a member of their Board of Directors. The facility was, and still is, a kill shelter, which means due to the large number of animal coming into the facility and few number of adoption opportunities the shelter could only kennel a percent of animal for a limited time. The reality is that more animals were euthanized than adopted. Though it was not what Bonnie believed, she accepted reality.

Any change starts with small steps, so her first step was to try to find homes for all the golden retrievers coming into this facility. She did not want to see a single golden retriever euthanized on her watch. That is what led to our first adult dog adoption, Liz.

Liz, like any adult adopted or fostered animal, came with months to years of pre-programed experiences, most of which created bad habits. Working with a mature adopted or fostered dog means training isn't as easy, as with a puppy. Training becomes more complicated while trying to understand the obstacles in the path of the animal's learning. You will learn more about Liz in a later chapter. The important point is that this led us to become a foster home for Golden Retrieve Rescue, which means we would bring in rescue dogs in need of a short term home, till a suitable permanent home is found for them to be adopted. While we house these foster pets, we try to make them more adoptable by improving their appearance through baths, nutritious food, and exercise. A dog also becomes more attractive, to potential adoptees, if they have obedience training. When a dog dutifully responds to sit, down, stay, come, etc. they find homes faster.

So for years we have had foster dogs added to and departing from our pack of dogs several times per year, which also adds another level of learning about group dynamics. These changes are a wonderful learning experience for a dog trainer because every time a new member is added or departs the pack, the dynamics and relationships among all of the members of the pack change. This is where my learning was accelerated. Taking the knowledge from the books and articles I read, I was then implementing this new knowledge to the variety of pack members, which was an amazing learning experience. It was easy to then implement similar techniques through observation or intervention with humans in a variety of organizations.

Working with a wide variety of dogs from puppies to rescues to foster's has led me to earning an assortment of titles with my teammates in obedience, rally, agility, and tracking. The success enjoyed in dog show competition, then provided me to the opportunity to become an obedience and rally dog show judge. Once again, the experience observing the team work of human-dog interaction, in competitive events, added more knowledge to my tool box.

In my professional career, which has spanned more than 40 years in sales and sales management, I have worked for 11 companies, started two businesses and owned a pet store. During this time, I've observed a wide variety of management styles, corporate structures, and the results produced by the many different leadership styles. What I have found is the organizations that embrace philosophies similar to those employed by progressive animal trainers tended to have the strong company morale, sincere and customer

24

responsive customer service staff, highest employee retention, and experience long term, consistent growth.

I have taught classes in the School of Business and Department of Marketing at University of Northern Iowa and Eastern Michigan University.

In addition, for over 20 years I have been a public speaker at conventions, business meetings, and business associations on topic such as:

How to Treat You Employees like a Dog

Who Moved My Dog Dish

Overheads and Golden Retrievers

In Dog Years

Selling Like a Dog

Pack Behavior

Don't Bark

Best in Show

Job One

These are presentations that each focus on activity of life that most people participate in doing on a daily basis. Or behavior people had practiced but, for some reason got out of the habit. The purpose of this book is to remind you of such daily activities; or if you are already doing these things encourage you to continue doing these activities; or introduce you to new ways of doing these activities. Most of these are basic activities people use daily. If not this is will be an opportunity to learn some fundamental skills.

In many of these experiences I have been accompanied by one of my dogs who assist in the presentations.

This book is the culmination of what I have learned over 20 years of doing these programs.

My teaching style relates a learning experience to stories, and I use stories to illustrate a specific point. Each of the following chapters in this book is made up of two stories followed by a common lesson. Each of the chapters in this book will open with a dog story, followed by a similar human story, and finish with an explanation tying the two together. I have also found that it is important to keep written communication short, to the point, and contain a message. Hopefully you will find that the following stories are easy to read, make sense, and provide a useful lesson.

The opening of each chapter begins with true a story of a dog that has been part of my pack. Chapters are named for the featured character whose story introduces the chapters learning subject material. The names of the dogs in this book have not been changed or altered. These are real dogs, some were adopted as puppies and lived with us their entire life; others were rescues, adopted as adults, who also lived the rest of their lives as member of our pack; and some were dogs we fostered and only lived in our pack several months. I have taken the real-life learning experiences from living with these dogs to illustrate a leadership teaching opportunity.

The second story in each chapter is about people I have met or worked with throughout my professional career. In these cases, I have changed the names of the people. In most cases, these human stories are a conglomeration of behaviors observed by several people who possess similar traits in like positions. They may be considered as stereotypical activities of real people I have observed.

If you have spent any time working in business or in any organization, I am sure you will recognize many of the traits these people exhibit. Most display very common characteristics found within members of virtually every organization. Some are more extreme than others. Most people see such human behaviors, but they do not understand why such behavior is occurring and even more important how to work with people acting with such behavior.

The success of any organization is directly related to what behaviors are tolerated, encouraged, or extinguished. We all come from different life experiences and are products of the environment in which we were raised. Each of us is the culmination of people we have met in our life and the decisions we have made. The behaviors a person has displayed in their life and how that behavior has been rewarded, discouraged, or extinguished is now displayed in their future relationship with others.

The third component of each chapter will describe the common characteristics of the dogs and humans discussed earlier in that chapter. I will then explain how to deal with such behavioral traits. Why or how either the dog or human developed such behavior. This segment of the chapter will also explain the training needed to correct, or encourage the behaviors displayed by both the dog and human described in that chapter.

If I am successful, you will learn how to become a better dog trainer, parent, spouse, or leader. Since we use the same skills to train a dog; as are found in business developing employees or co-workers; raising a child; or build a successful relationship with a spouse/significant other. I will demonstrate common traits that both dogs and humans possess. After reading this book, I'm certain you will be able to better recognize specific dog and/or human behavior when you see it. Then you will have more tools to know how to handle both human and dog behaviors.

You will learn how your behaviors influence other people to continue their current behavior; extinguish undesirable behavior of others, or equally important, knowing when changing the behavior of others people is not possible.

The skills needed to lead an organization, raise a child, build a harmonious marriage, or train a dog, are the same traits. As you read the following chapters you will become familiar with these skills. They are simple basic activities that will be expanded upon throughout the remainder of this book.

If you want to evaluate a person's leadership skills, give them an 8-week-old puppy and return in six months.

If the puppy is scared and cowering, you have an autocratic manager.

If the puppy is running free and wild doing whatever it wants, you have a laissez-faire manager.

If the puppy is reluctantly responsive to commands, you have a democratic manager.

If the puppy is enthusiastically involved with the human trainer, happily taking direction, you have a found a leader.

Your behavior towards others, trains them how to treat you in the future.

**If you help other people achieve their goal
you will achieve your goal.**

Chapter Two

CINDI

Early in our marriage, for a Valentine's Day gift, I bought my wife, Bonnie, a female Golden Retriever puppy we named Cindi. At the time, we had just one other dog Sonny who was an 8 year old, male Golden Retriever, that Bonnie had since he was 8 weeks old.

Sonny lived his life as the only dog in the house, so we weren't sure how he would respond to the new puppy. He had always been very friendly with both people and dogs, so it was expected the new puppy would not cause him any problems. Our next-door neighbors had an older yellow lab, Missy, who also had spent her life as an only dog in their family. Missy was a bit of a character, not a problem child, but she had a mischievous side.

We lived in a neighborhood that might be termed as rural suburbia, where the lots were about two acres each. The yards were open without any fences, and the streets were unpaved dirt roads. The surrounding area to this small housing development was mostly farmland. I provide this description to the neighborhood to explain one of Missy's favorite activities. Missy was an indoor dog; she was only outside when the neighbors were outside with her. On weekends when they would spend hours outside doing yard work, Missy was outside with them and she was very good about staying in her own yard, most of the time – except if it was a hot day and if no one was watching. Missy would slip away to a nearby pond, filled with swampy water, just to cool down. After a good cooling swim, she would return home very proud of herself, wet, filthy, and smelling like a swamp, which then led to a reprimand, lecture, and a bath.

So, she knew the swamp was off limits, but she was not to be deterred from future attempts to visit the swamp. Surrounding neighbors were aware of Missy's exploits. So, when she was seen heading to the swamp, and caught by a neighbor we knew to redirect her back home, which she very reluctantly obeyed. But she learned from past failures to calculate a route providing her with the best chances of achieving her goal of swamp swimming. Missy would work her way to the swamp by staying close to neighbor's houses, moving between the shrubs and houses, so we could not spot her out of our windows. She proved to be very calculated and stealthy. I share this story to demonstrate how smart a dog Missy was.

About the same time we got Cindi, Missy was 13 years old and her owners were getting concerned she was becoming lethargic and cranky. She seemed to have given up on living, and her days were spent sleeping. As with many of her other mischievous behaviors, she hadn't tried to sneak off to the swamp in quite a while. Missy's owners had spoken to us on several occasions concerned about how much longer Missy would live. So when we first introduced Missy to Cindi, the neighbors were worried Missy might not be friendly.

We were all cautiously hoping the young puppy would be respectful of the older Missy, and kept a close watch when they were together. Interestingly enough, the opposite was the case. The lethargic-cranky old Yellow Labrador became energized and protective of the new neighbor Cindi. Missy became maternal and

Cindi understood. Cindi would follow Missy around and they became best friends. The older dog was constantly teaching Cindi how to behave; and where the yard boundaries were. And, Cindi learned by example – mimicking Missy's actions. When Cindi's behavior needed to be corrected Missy did this as well. It was an amazing friendship putting new life and energy into an old dog who just months earlier had looked like her days were numbered.

Everybody needs a job.

Missy now had a purpose in her life, to train Cindi. Cindi recognized this older, much larger dog as her teacher and friend who helped her through puppyhood. If Missy was outside and Cindi was inside, Missy would come to our house looking for her pupil. They greeted each other like best buddies. The responsibility of raising Cindi probably extended Missy's life. And, it certainly made her last years more fun. Plus, when Missy felt it was the appropriate time, she even tried to show Cindi how to sneak down to the swamp.

Older dogs like to teach younger dogs.

Several years later, we added another female Golden Retriever puppy to our pack named Heidi, and Cindi took on the role of the new puppy's teacher, just as Missy had done for her years before. Heidi looked up to Cindi, similar to the way Cindi had looked up to Missy. Heidi followed Cindi in the same manner Cindi had followed Missy. They were best buddies.

Missy had taught her well.

After 30 years of living with dogs, I have learned new members of our pack learn much faster from the older experience canine pack member than from the human members.

RONNIE

Ronnie owned a small manufacturing company, which he'd purchased from his father. Since it was a family-owned business, Ronnie had started working there at a young age, learning the business inside and out. So, he was thoroughly knowledgeable about all facets of the company.

Over the years, Ronnie had numerous employees leave and start their own manufacturing businesses. He never viewed these departures as a threat, rather maintained friendships with these former employees. I never worked for Ronnie nor had I ever worked for any of his former employees, but several were long-time friends of mine who always spoke of Ronnie with the utmost respect.

Many of these former employees had become actively involved with trade associations representing their profession, and these people all attributed their success to Ronnie's mentoring. He was always teaching and with every new employee in his company, Ronnie took it upon himself to initiate the training. He would meet with each newly hired employee after they had completed their new hire human resource documents, to begin the training process.

Knowing the business as well as Ronnie did, he would show the new employee how to do a foundation task associated with their new job and break the task into small increments. Ronnie would begin with an explanation of the task he wanted the new employee to learn, and why it was important. Ronnie would not just explain the specific task the employee was to perform, but also the ultimate result.

He would demonstrate how the task was to be completed and explain in detail the steps involved while performing the task. He would do this several times to make sure the new employee understood the steps involved before turning the task over to the new hire. Ronnie would back away and observe while the new employee performed the task and only provide feedback if requested. While the trainee was performing the task for the first time, Ronnie would step back and quietly observe how the task was carried out. Providing feedback only after the trainee had completed the task uninterrupted.

Feedback from Ronnie was always presents constructive and encouraging.

Feedback is critical to learning

After offering the new hire his observations, Ronnie would give the new employee the opportunity to do the task again, and just as he did the first time, Ronnie would stand back to observe the new hire's technique. Once the task was completed, he'd once again provide constructive feedback. When Ronnie felt the new hire had the basic understanding and skills to properly perform the given task, he would leave the new hires work area with an assignment specific to the newly taught task. The technique Ronnie was using to teach his new employees is called Social Learning Theory.

Leaders are constantly teaching.

Social learning theory is the most effective method of teaching a new skill and it is a four-step process, the first is to explain the task to be learned. In this initial explanation, the trainee is told why this task is important. The trainer breaks the task down into small easy-to-explain steps. In some cases, there might be manual or written instructions as to how a task is performed. In either case, the student first receives an explanation.

During the second step, the mentor physically demonstrates how to perform the task. Once the mentor believes the student understands the process, then in step three they are given the opportunity to perform the task. While the student performs the task, the mentor closely observes the student's technique. Then in step four the mentor provides feedback to the student. Steps three and four are repeated until the mentor is confident the student has learned the task.

Social Learning Theory
1. Explain what you want the person to learn
2. Show the person what you want them to learn
3. Let them perform the exercise
4. Provide the trainee with feedback

After several days, Ronnie would return to observe the complete work and ability of the new hire at the newly taught task. This visit had a purpose. After giving the new hire time to practice the new skill, Ronnie wanted to provide the new hire with feedback. When Ronnie was confident the new hire was proficient with the new skill, he would then teach the next step in the work process. Ronnie would go through the same training steps: explain what needed to be performed, demonstrate the proper technique for performing the task, allows the trainee to perform the task, and then provide feedback at each stage of a new task.

People do what you inspect; not what you expect.

This treatment for new employees was not a sometimes behavior or special treatment for selected employees; it was an every employee way of life for Ronnie. His attention to training employees was not just when he first started his company or for select occasions when he had excess time, Ronnie believed his most important responsibility was teaching.

Foundation skills are critical to building a team.

Ronnie believed the training of new employees was similar to building a house. If time is invested at the beginning to ensure the foundation is properly laid, everything gets easier. In the case of building a house foundation, if time is spent upfront ensuring everything is level and square, by the time construction gets to the second floor, it is far more likely the building will continue to be square and level. But if time is not invested early, while constructing the foundation, by the time construction gets to the second floor the walls will not be square and the floor will not be level. Small rooms on higher floors will exhibit a distorted appearance – which is quickly realized if you are trying to wallpaper the room!

Comparing this analogy to employees, Ronnie believed if he put the time into training foundational skills they would ensure the company's future product would continue to exhibit the company's history of high quality. Ronnie also believed the time invested up front with all new employees would in the long term provide him with more time to do other things, because he would not have to fix mistakes. Honnie believed the more his employees learned, the more he would be relieved from doing these tasks; allowing him the more time to learn new things. Ronnie had a strong commitment to learn a skill; teach a skill; and learn another new skill.

Training involves small steps

Ronnie leadership had another interesting leadership trait, he was commonly the last person to leave the building at the end of the day, and he had a habit of walking around the building to see what people were working on. On these evening walk arounds he would look at finished products ready for shipment and inspect the workmanship. While walking around he would look at work in progress to inspect for quality and consistency. This inspection of work included office employees, looking at what paper work was on their desk and prepared reports. Getting a sense of how the company was functioning by looking around. When he found situations not looking correct or caused a question, Ronnie would simply leave a post-it note on the workbench or desk where he had a question. Such notes would simply say see me in the morning or I have a question. Sometimes it was a misunderstanding other times it was a need for training or re-training. Ronnie kept communication open and organizational structure flat. He believed that people do what you inspect not what you expect.

Critical components of learning:

The first step is to establish what needs to be learned. What is the purpose for this training program and what do you want the participants to have at the conclusion which they do not possess at the beginning?

Training is different than education. Education exposes the participants to information. Education provides them with the awareness of options and alternatives. Training, on the other hand, teaches specific skills. Training programs are established to teach the participant how to perform a task. Training for the purpose of training is a nice way to spend time, but it doesn't improve the needs of the participants or the organization.

Taking time to analyze the real needs of the organization and the participants is a critical first step.

Great leaders create an environment to help their employees do their job better.

Employees fail at their jobs because they either do not possess the mental or physical skills or because they were not properly trained and equipped to do the job.

Ronnie understood the importance of foundation skills and training these skills in small steps. Such behavior has been displayed by other leaders.

Good teachers/leaders are hard to come by.

For example the first practice of each season from 1948 to 1975 for the UCLA's Men's Basketball team, it was always the same, John Wooden, the UCLA head basketball coach, had won 10 NCAA Division I National Championships over a 12-year span 1964-1975, Wooden would bring his players together in a huddle around him as he sat on a chair, then he would begin practice by teaching them the proper way to put their socks and shoes on. He would methodically take a clean, white cotton sock and pull it slowly, very neatly over his right foot and smooth out any wrinkles. He made sure the heel pocket was centered, and the toe of the sock properly aligned with the toes inside. He would then duplicate the same procedure with his left foot and sock.

Next Coach Wooden would move to the right shoe, loosening the laces so his foot would easily slide into it. He would ensure his foot was properly aligned in the shoe and only then did he begin tightening the laces closest to the toe. He'd progress to the next eyelets and tightened the laces. He wanted to be sure they were not too tight or too loose and then continue lacing up his right shoe until he arriving at the top eyelets. The finale came when he would tie a perfect bow knot with the correct pressure. Next he would repeat the exact same procedure with the left shoe and foot following the same meticulous steps.

This would conclude the first team practice, emphasizing the importance of foundation skills.

In another example, before going to battle, the great Admiral Bull Halsey, leader of the United States Naval Pacific Fleet during World War II, would pull out and open a small wooden box he kept in his office containing one multi-folded sheet of paper. He would unfold the paper and read its contents. In very simple print was a valuable message: Starboard – Right; Port – Left.

When asked, Admiral Halsey said reading the note reminded him in battle stay focused on the fundamentals.

The Japanese have a saying that battles are won by the side that making the fewest mistakes. In other words, do not over think or complicate the task; keep it simple. Follow foundation skills.

Learn a skill, teach a skill, and learn a new skill.

Many companies do not recognize the importance of cross-training culture. Constant learning and training keeps people engaged; sharing knowledge and skills is contagious. Employees who were particularly good at a skill should watch for other employees with whom to share their skill so they, too, can learn a new skill. To move into a position requiring new skills, the company has to first have the staff to backfill the position being vacated. Too often organizations promote an individual to a position of greater responsibility without considering who will fill the void left by the promotion, until it is too late. When such promotions take place, without considering the impact of the newly created vacancy, remaining staff is then overloaded and having to fulfill an additional job the company is not prepared to handle.

Leaders make everyone else around them better.

In Ronnie's company, part of the motivation to train others was if others were not available or capable of doing your job, then the person was not able to be promoted. Some organizations might call this cross training, but it was just the accepted work culture in Ronnie's company. Ronnie was always looking for staff to learn parts of his job so he could learn something new. Growing organizations are capable of constantly implementing new and different programs because they have staff who are both motivated and competent to learn new skills.

I have been in organizations where the culture was just the opposite, people unwilling to share skills and knowledge for fear someone else might take their job. Organizations where employees hoard knowledge, and are unwilling to teach and share learned skills with other staff members become stagnate, will soon to fall behind their competitors creating a death spiral.

Role models and mentors

Those we chose as role models are the type of people that we want to emulate. Role models create an image for us to copy and act like. Many times, we never physically meet our role model, such as the frequent references to high-profile celebrities such as sports stars and movie stars as role models. There are many examples as to the impact, high-profile celebrities can have on the clothes worn by the mass population, or the sunglasses worn, or the behavior their public will try to imitate. Whether it is the physical appearance we would like to have, or the education we would like to have, or job we would like to have, role models are important because they provide a blue print of what we want to achieve.

Role models give us something to aspire toward, hopefully in a positive manner. We all have role models. We all have someone who we want to be like for the way they look, act or what they have achieved. Our role models will change as we age, but we all have them. Even the biggest celebrities have role models who they are trying to emulate. This is proven over and over when high-profile celebrities are interviewed and asked about the influences in their lives. For example, there are professional athletes who wear a particular jersey number because this was the number worn by their role model. They will tell the story of a person who they held in esteem

41

and wanted to fashion their life after. In many cases, a role model provides motivation to work hard in an effort to achieve the same success.

Examples are the best teachers in life

It is important to realize we have role models and to understand how these role models are influencing our lives and behavior. In most cases, role models do not realize who or how many people view them in this position of respect. Equally important is the understanding that others may be looking at you as their role model. Regardless who you are, every day your behavior is constantly viewed by others. Then such behavior is replicated by those who view you as their role model. The people who view you as a role model could be your children, grandchildren, neighbors child, co-workers, or subordinates, you may not know who or how many others look up to you and want to be like you.

Whether you view yourself as a role model or not, too few people understand that their behavior is constantly being scrutinized. How you look and act, also influences how others treat you.

Mentors are different than role models. Mentors are teachers. They are the people in our lives who teach us how to behave. We all need people in our lives that will provide us with instruction and helping us to achieve our goals. When we are young, our mentor could be a family member, teacher, neighbor or family friend. On a frequent basis, high-profile people such as professional athletes, college athletes, television celebrities, tell stories of how their lives have been changed or directed by a mentor in their lives.

Mentors are very important because they impart knowledge. Whether people realize it or not, most mentor-student relationships frequently involve the use of Social Learning Theory technique. They teach values to us when we are young through explanation followed by demonstration, observation and feedback. As we get older, mentors more often come from an artificial pack, someone we meet at work, in the military, at college, or in a variety of other locations.

As a child, a mentor is usually someone we have frequent access to, but as we get older our mentor may live a distance away.

When we are younger, we are likely to have one or very few who act as mentors in our lives. As we get older we are less likely to be limited in having just one mentor at a time, but just the opposite – most of us have a variety of mentors. Later in life mentors provide more of a sounding board for us. This is important because each of us is the only person who can solve our own problems. Mentors give us counsel to turn to when we have a decision to make. They are trusted sources of advice who have earned our respect.

We all need to have mentors in our lives because they help us make better decisions that directly impact our lives. Equally important, we need to be a mentor to others. Mentors and mentored have a unique symbiotic relationship, like Missy and Cindi. Missy's attitude on life was changed with the introduction of Cindi. Cindi's development was enhanced by Missy's leadership.

Technical Skills vs Social Skills

There are two functional skills that humans utilize on a daily basis; we are born with the foundations of both, they are then developed throughout life with the help of others. The first skill is the more innate of the two; it is in our DNA at birth, more so than the second skill. The second skill requires more experiential learning either from mentoring of others or observation of role models.

We are born with technical skills such as artistic, musical, mechanical or creative talent. People born with such talent perform such activities naturally. These are people who at a young age can sing on key and naturally harmonize with others. These are people who can pick up a musical instrument for the first times, spend several hours on their own understanding how it works, then begin playing music. As compared to someone who is not born with musical talent and spends years taking musical lessons, but still unable to make anything sounding like music. Or children who are born with natural artistic or mechanical skills who are able create their own toys at a very young age without the benefit of instructions or manuals, using the common simple items within their surroundings. Yet many other have access to those same items and never consider making such innovative creations.

Those who are born with technical skills, such the ability to sing, paint, design, or build these skills can always be improved through the help of others. Where such technical skills take an individual many times depend on the opportunities presented in life. A person born with mechanical skills whose father is a carpenter might provide a strong drive to follow that profession. That same individual if exposed early in life to different opportunities might instead become an orthopedic surgeon. The technical skill a person is born with is raw talent. Early life experiences often have a powerful influence as to how these inborn technical skills are utilized later in life. At a young age the opportunities and decision regarding how one utilizes technical skills often impacts where we go with the rest of life.

The second skill is that of social interaction, it is not brought to us as much via our DNA but rather it is more a learned skill. Social skills are not as innate, yet there is some genetic predisposition to social skill, which we are either born with or not. Whether a person is introverted or extroverted; leader or follower; is part of their genetic make-up at birth. Leaders are born, but what leaders do with such skills many times requires the nurturing of others.

Early in life someone or somebodies teach us how to interact with others. These are either through lessons taught by mentors in our live or experiences we have observed watching our role models. Most of our social skills are developed as a result of early life experiences,

44

either through a purposeful training of others, or from natural observation of how people interact.

Social skills include such activities as how to meet and greet others. How to give compliments, or not; how to accept recognition are taught skills. How to treat other who are in positions viewed as subordinates, peers or superior is a learned skill. How a person behaves in public is a learned at an early age and build upon throughout life as a result of mentors and observation.

Technical skills, which come natural, are what most of people use to start their careers. The technical skills we are born with usually play a part obtaining entry level positions. Most entry level jobs are more dependent on technical skills and less social skills. But as people progress to positions of greater responsibility in an organization it is usually due to their social skills. The ability to build relationships with co-workers or customers provides them opportunities to take on new responsibilities.

Both Missy and Ronnie displayed an array of technical and social skills, some of which may have been part of their DNA at birth; but even more of these skills were developed through the help of others. Both used their social skills to build a mentor relationship with those younger than themselves helping their new protégé to fine tune job related technical skills while also teaching the social skills of life. Those people who have learned how to put others needs in front of their own will receive the commitment of others.

Boomerang Worker

Missy is an example of how everyone needs a job. When Cindi was introduced into Missy's life her demeanor change, she now had a new purpose. Having a purpose contributes to a dog or persons mental and physical health.

So often we put time limits, age or quotas on people. Someone hits a certain age and it is time for them to retire. When a company needs to become more profitable one of the options they execute a program of early retirement of the highest paid employees. This also means losing some of the most qualified, talented people in the company. Those people who have retired and then return to work has created a new category of workers, called the Boomerang Workers. Society for Human Resources reports 30% of US companies have re-hired retired employees. They also report that one third of employees who accepted early retirement programs are back to their previous job within a year. Over 50% of the employees in high tech organization such as Aerospace are 50 years old or older. An organizations culture is often produced by long tenured employees.

The most qualified person for a job may be someone with years of experience, rather than, or in addition to job skills. Certain skills such as technical skills are more easily transferable. Younger employees usually show up with more technical skills than social skills. They typically are interested to learn new technical skills, which mean they learn such skill quickly. Skills versus experience are two very different forms of knowledge. Learning to do a job, mastering the technical skills to perform a job, is very different than obtaining years of experience working with people or projects.

Knowledge from experience is why older managers or head coaches will make decisions in an important game that is not what most would predict or expect to have done. They had a "gut feeling" that in turn led to a game winning decision. Experience is also seen in the variety of techniques employed in practice and proofing. Experience also provides the older leader an insight into reading their players.

The average age of World Series winning head manager 2007-2016 was 57.6 years old and five of those winning managers were over the age of 60.

From 2008 -2017 five of the Super Bowl winning coaches were over 60 at the time they won. Bill Belichick, New England

Patriots head coach, the only head coach in the NFL to win five super bowls, winning his fifth in 2017 at the age of 64, the second oldest coach in the NFL that season. The oldest coach during the 2016-2017 season was Pete Carroll who was 65 years old and whose team won the Super Bowl three years earlier, at age 62 years old. Both of these coaches enjoyed more success as head coaches after the age of 55 year old than they did before the age of 55 years old.

Do your job
Do your job well
Teach others your job

Bill Belichick
Head coach
New England Patriots football team

Anything can be accomplished; if no one worries about who gets credit.

Chapter Three

Heidi

Heidi is the puppy described in the introduction chapter as the reason that I became involved in the crazy dog training world.

Most of the other dogs described in this book came into my life, as rescues, when they were a year old or older. As rescues, who knows what their breeding had been or what experiences they had before coming into my life. In general, rescue dogs do not make particularly good performance dogs. There are always exceptions, but a solid foundation as a puppy provides the best building blocks for a successful performance dog.

The most important learning phase in a dog's life is the first 12 weeks after birth and the experiences during this time-frame remains for the rest of the dog's life or it is very difficult to re-program. The highest accomplished dogs in competitive performance events are bred for the sport that they will compete and subsequently receive extensive training during the most formative 12 weeks of life. Competitive dog trainers select specific lines of obedience dogs they want to breed and become involved in the puppy's training immediately after birth to help produce the desired behaviors.

Heidi was the puppy we received as a gift from a highly respected breeder of Golden Retrievers. Heidi came from a line of Golden Retrievers bred specifically for obedience. She was an incredibly intelligent dog and she wanted to learn, but she needed a skilled teacher. In other words, she knew more about dog obedience than I did because I did not have the training or experience to train a dog for obedience.

Heidi had a pedigree providing her with the skills to learn and please. Equally important, her first eight weeks of life were under the direct supervision of a breeder, who understood the importance of puppy training. During those formative first eight weeks, Heidi had daily exposure to people and a well-organized puppy development program, which the breeder had perfected through years of research and work. This gave Heidi a leg up on any of the future rescues we would own.

Normally Bonnie did all of the dog training in our pack. But the timing of this puppy's arrival was not good, since Bonnie had just opened our new retail venture Pet Outfitters. So, Heidi ended up with me as the trainer and team mate for future performance events.

As stated earlier, rescue dogs do not make particularly good performance dogs, but there are always exceptions. Similarly, hiring the best human for a job is dependent on their pedigree, previous training and experience. Knowing how to select the correct person for a specific job and the skills needed for that job goes a long way in that person's success, which in turns then contributes to the organizations success.

So let's pick up the story from the time I attended my first one-day, eight-hour seminar on dog obedience (the introduction chapter). After a day of listening to this famous dog trainer explain motivational and training theories, that were the same lessons I had learned while working on my MSOD Degree, I was hooked on using this knowledge to train Heidi.

Now working with Heidi, for someone with a degree in MSOD, the process was like a chemist working in a laboratory. This was the good news. The bad news was I did not possess the tools (knowledge or skills) to properly bring out the best performance in the dog I had. Heidi was like a high-performance Indy race car and I was a 16-year-old boy who had just taken his first driver's training class. She wanted to learn at the level of a PhD at 200 mph and I had the depth of knowledge of a kindergartener on a tricycle.

At this point I would be considered an unconscious – incompetent, since I did not possess the skills needed to train Heidi (incompetent) and I did not realize how uninformed I was (unconscious). Before my learning could begin I had to become aware of what I needed to know.

When I enthusiastically returned home from the all-day, dog obedience seminar Bonnie realized I was excited to train Heidi but still did not possess the skillset to perform the job. In other words, I needed a lot of help to take the next step in dog training. As is typically the case, Bonnie knew best what needed to be done. She enrolled me in a weekly dog training class in the basement of a Catholic church in downtown Denver.

Since I was not available to attend dog training classes on weekdays, which is when most dog training classes are offered, and because I was a full-time sales manager who spent most week days traveling all over the country working with sales people calling on customers, Bonnie found a class which met on Saturdays. Two nuns taught the class and were assisted by two wannabee nuns, (not really, they just acted really tough, like the nuns.) Before the human trainers could bring our dogs to class, we had to learn specific foot work. We had to perfect a skill called "heeling". Heeling is a dog-handler team exercise requiring the dog to be positioned on the left side of the handler, facing the same direction, with the dog's nose to shoulder in alignment with the handlers hip. For the handler this exercise involves

51

walking in a direction while the dog stays in the heel position, left side aligned with the handler hip. It is helpful to the dog when the handler has accurate footwork. So it is important for handlers to knowing exactly where to place each foot walking straight as well as when making either a left or a right a turn, 180-degree about turns or performing figure eights.

The instructors were really strict about using the exact footwork. In fact, the nuns were so fanatical about foot work they had rubber mats on the floor with painted foot prints for handlers to follow. We humans practiced placing each step in the proper place, over and over. After the human students learned the foot work, next we had to perform the foot work to the beat of a metronome to develop-military like footwork at a consistent rhythm. The human teammate had to perform these exercises repeatedly, consistently and precisely. Once mastered without the dog, then the humans were allowed to bring their dogs to class.

At this point I am moving from being an unconscious – incompetent to a conscious – incompetent. I am beginning to realize (becoming conscious) how much I did not know, but I still did not have the skills to perform the exercises.

Foundation skills are critical to building long-term success.

I am sure you have already figured out I was the last human member of the class who was allowed to bring his dog to class. In retrospect, the nuns were wonderful. They were what I needed to keep me from doing everything my own way which would have been incorrect confusing to my dog. The nuns taught me the foundation of more than just dog training. The lessons learned in dog class were useful in many other parts of my life – for starters, success is built on a strong foundation. In all aspects of life, most people want to skip the boring foundation skills and rush into the more fun activities.

But dog training begins with teaching the person (handler) the skills before the handler can teach the dog the exercises. Once Heidi was added to the team we got much better. Since she'd been bred to be an obedience dog, she understood her job. And Heidi more than made up for my lack of dog training knowledge and ability. The nuns would watch this dog perform her portion of the exercises perfectly while I fumbled with my footwork, dropped the leash and tried to follow directions, and looked totally confused. They would shake their heads watching two members of what was supposed to be the same team performing at opposing ends of the learning spectrum. They had no hesitation expressing their very blunt thoughts about my lack of talent stated quite loudly.

This was the point where reward, reprimand and motivation were introduced. One of the most important skills of a dog trainer is to create an environment for success. This is the ability to recognize and immediately reward desired behaviors. Most commonly, the reward for a dog performing correctly is a bit of food. But it can also be a toy, praise, or verbal recognition. As a trainer, the timing of the dog's reward is important. It must be prompt, and consistent. To create a consistent behavior by a dog it is important when you find the dog doing something correctly, to reward correct behavior immediately, with praise and food.

As a trainer it is important to understand what the dog values as a reward. The more valuable the reward is perceived by the dog, the more motivated the dog is to produce the desired behavior. High valued rewards are used when a new behavior is initiated because this maximizes the dog's attention. After a behavior becomes consistent, a less valued reward can be used to reinforce this behavior.

For example, when I started to teach Heidi to heel on my left side, I would use microwaved hot dog bits which were really tasty. As she learned the exercise and got consistent, I substituted small kibbles of her dog food, more nutritious, less fat, but more familiar and not as exciting.

As our dog-human teamwork improved, and we functioned more like a team I wanted to test our skills in a competitive event. Obedience dog trials take place on weekends allowing teams of dog and humans to show off their skills. They perform a pre-determined set of exercises, which are then scored by experienced judges. The judge's scores are tallied to determine the first, second, third and fourth place finishers. A minimum score must be achieved to qualify and teams must qualify three times to attain a title. A wide variety of titles are available to be earned based on the exercises performed and the level of team's skills.

Heidi and I showed on the first (lowest) level called Novice and it was not pretty. I was clueless, but Heidi, as she had done in class, made me look good. We qualified and I thought I was the coolest person in the world. It was a two-day show, Saturday and Sunday, so of course I registered for both days. On Sunday, we qualified again – Heidi looking in total control and me bobbling my way through the exercises.

Now I had progressed to the level of a conscious – competent, I was aware of the task I needed to perform, and though clumsy I could perform those tasks. I now possessed the skills of training and leading the team (competent), but I had to constantly think about all of the small details of every exercise (conscious) such as each step I took in the heeling pattern. At this level none of the exercises came naturally, I had to think about every little thing I was doing.

Our success caused me to become even more obsessed to learn more about dog training. I wanted to improve our performance and achieve higher scores. I needed to better understand my job as a teammate because Heidi could only be as good as her teammate. I needed to create a training schedule. I needed to improve my handling skills by practicing and having more experienced trainers, teachers, and coaches, provide feedback. I could not do it myself. I knew I needed the help of people who had knowledge and experience I did not possess. I knew if I improved, our team would become much more successful.

When you are winning, it is because of the dog;
When you are losing it is because of the handler.

Before Heidi was two years old, we earned our first level Novice Title and our second level Open Title, picking up several first places on the way. Due to an autoimmune disease, Heidi's show career was cut short at age two. She did live a comfortable life working at Pet Outfitters till age nine, when she died of liver disease.

CUSTOMER SERVICE AND TECH REPS.

At the same time I was training Heidi, I took a new job as National Accounts Manager for a manufacturer of medical equipment. Their traditional customers had been many small, local, independent companies who were now selling their businesses to larger companies, (also known as consolidators) creating large multi-branch national organizations. Due to the consolidation of small independently owned business, who had been the primary customers, of my new employer, a new sales direction was now needed.

Consolidation is a common occurrence when an industry enters the mature phase of a life cycle. It also means a change in handling these newly created customers. Multi-branch National Companies are large bureaucratic organizations with layers of staff, which create barriers to access. My employer had built a business selling to small individually owned companies which provided easy access and familiar rapport by local sales representatives. The new large multi-branch national companies required sales at a corporate office level. Selling to this kind of customer was a very different environment for not only my new employer, but also for our competitors.

I am not a very technically gifted person. I did not understand the products I was selling, how they were made, maintained, or even how they were used. In addition, I had very limited knowledge of the customer base for these products. These are all technical skills which can be taught. What I had that my new employer needed was the knowledge and experience selling to large corporations and obtaining access to C-level executives (i.e. **C**EO, **C**FO, **C**OO, etc.).

I was missing the technical product knowledge to do my job and I had a lot of learning in front of me. Like my experience with Heidi, at this point, I was an unconscious – incompetent. But unlike my experience with Heidi I had to do the training on my own, without the discipline of the nuns.

As luck would have it, my office was located right outside of the customer service and technical service bull pen area. The two support staffs were located in work cubicles next to each other, which worked really well, since much of their work was intertwined. My first order of business was learning about the products I would be selling. I received the typical tour of manufacturing plant then met staff and got a general overview of the company. But the critical components I really needed to learn was the knowledge possessed by the staff located right outside my office door. I learned more by sitting in my office listening to them talk to each other about customers and customer problems. I soon moved a chair out of my office and into the cubicle bullpen area listening and asking questions.

Between phone calls that the customer service and technical service representatives were taking from customers, I would ask them questions which were then answered by a variety of people in these two departments. This was a great learning experience. Customer service representatives knew customers, their names, locations, sales, etc. The technical representatives knew the technical aspects of the products we manufactured such as maintenance, repair, components, etc. As noted earlier in this chapter, I am not a patient person so after a couple weeks in the office I needed to get out and visit customers.

Having read through the product catalog and manuals, as well as, having listened to the talented customer service and technical service staff, I was ready to go. My first sales calls made me aware of how complex the products were and my two weeks of training was not going to be enough. During my first week of sales calls, I spent more time on the phone with product questions for my trainers, tech service and customer service staff. This is where I was transforming from an unconscious-incompetent to a conscious-incompetent.

From this point on, I took one of the customer service or technical service representatives with me. I did mention that I am not patient. This, too, was eye opening, since traveling to call on customers was new experience for them. These are people who were great in their own environment, their cubical, but going into the customer's domain was a whole new experience. I had to figure out a way to get their knowledge and expertise in front of these very large customers to be successful.

This is when things got to be really fun. We each had strengths that the others did not possess. They were experts at the technical knowledge; I had the social and selling skills. I was not the product expert, the techs were and the customer service reps knew the customers. If I was to be successful, I needed to maximize these skills. I had spent my career traveling making sales calls. I was more comfortable on the road than in an office while the customer service and tech reps were just the opposite. I organized selling skills training programs for the support staff – teaching the skills of how to ask questions, identifying needs, gathering information, and product presentations. I also provided them with some of the practical travel knowledge I had learned from years of airports and hotel life.

It took a while to figure out how to use all of this talent. Customer service reps knew the intricacies of our ordering and delivery systems (more specifically purchasing and logistics). Tech reps knew the products, and I was responsible for selling the product. We then started setting up sales calls for each customer, specifically matching the company staff member with their most appropriate counter-part. For example, customer service reps were paired with members of the customer's purchasing department. Tech reps were teamed with repair centers and their personnel, who were responsible for repairing our products. My time was then spent providing the introductions, like being a match maker for two people on their first blind date. On the initial meeting I was the third person in the room handling introductions and directing conversation to begin building a relationship. I was also responsible for opening doors and securing final approvals with middle and upper management personnel.

As a three-member tag team, we each had our assigned departments based on the individual special skills. Each was prepared to collect particular information. By the end of these meetings, a stronger relationship existed between the respective departments each person met. We were now evolving from a sales person trying to get an order; to an external problem solver to help our customers improve their business.

Purchasing personnel liked having a customer service rep assigned to their account who they believed would improve continuity of service. It made it easier for the purchasing people because they did not have to start every telephone conversation explaining previous orders and issues. Repair center staff liked to have a friend at the manufacturer to help trouble-shoot problems, expedite repair parts delivery, etc. This was truly a win-win for everyone involved. It is a whole lot easier to call a friend for help, than a stranger.

People like buying from friends, not strangers.

At this point I was a conscious – competent, having to think about what we were doing, step by step, but able to perform my job in a productive manner.

At the conclusion of each day I traveled with tech service or customer service reps, making customer field trip visits, we would meet for dinner in the evening or breakfast the next morning to share what we had learned. The collected information was shared with team members and assembled in an organized matrix. After six months of customer field trips, the information we had gathered and organized from a variety of customers produced a really detailed picture of each major customer. Another unexpected benefit of the information we had gathered was a much better understanding of the entire industry we serviced. We had fine-tuned our program to the point we knew more about each of our major customers, regarding their use of our (and competitors) line of products, than they knew about themselves.

We knew their annual repair costs, average number of units in-service and out of service, comparative cost to repair or replace, etc. In addition, we learned a great deal of information about competitive products and how much each customer purchased of our products compared to each of our competitor's products. We learned the valued features of competitor's products, as well as each competitor's weaknesses. With all of this knowledge we now had become a sustained resource for each customer because we could help them improve efficiencies in their repair centers. We could help them make better repair to replace decisions. We weren't just selling products; we were a valuable business partner.

This success was the result of a team. It could never have been as accomplished by just one person, by myself. Utilizing each member's talents and knowledge we helped each other to succeed.

I should mention in the two years we implemented this program, company sales to these customers tripled, and total company sales double in three years. That is important because when I initiated customer sales calls which included customer service and technical service representatives I caught a lot of flax from upper management due to the expenses I was running up with sales calls involved two or three employees, which in turn increased costs. However those expenses were more than offset by increased sales, detail intelligence of our competitor's products, extensive market knowledge, and the intangibles of customer rapport. The staff who were now friends at our multi-branch national accounts were now as much a resource for our company personnel as we were for them.

Success is contagious

With the success of our tag-team sales calls, rapport was built with customers, and sales increased. Most importantly, because of the enthusiasm of tag-team members, others wanted to get involved. The knowledge obtained from repair centers was very useful for our company's repair center and its staff. This experience made the traveling tech reps into trainers for our company's repair department. The marketing department wanted to learn more about what customers perceived as strengthens and weaknesses of our competition, as well as, our own products. Future sales materials and advertising utilized the information gathered by this customer interaction. Our Engineering Department was interested to learn customer's comments which could then be used to improve our products and the creation of new products. At this point, the members of customer service and technical service departments had risen in recognition within our company.

**Leading people is about training the leader
how to be a teacher.**

Teamwork

Any great accomplishment in life requires the contributions of many working as a team. From the Wright Brothers and the first human flight to Roger Banisters, the first person to run a sub-four minute mile, it takes a team. We remember the name of Sir Edmond Hillary for being the first to reach the top of Mt. Everest or Neil Armstrong as the first to walk on the moon, but they were the fortunate namesakes of many people working together to make such accomplishments a reality. It is important to recognize, it takes a team to accomplish anything significant.

Asking others for help is not a sign of weakness, but rather a display of intelligence. If you have a goal and you can make an accurate assessment of the overall skills, talent, and knowledge needed to accomplish that goal; and then if you can honestly evaluate your own personal talent and skills as they apply to the pursuit of your goal, you will find many of the skills needed to achieve a desired outcome would be better performed by someone other than yourself.

Successful leaders like to surround themselves with people with diverse skills. They are not threatened by people who are smarter. Leaders are always teaching. They are always teaching others the skills to take their job. Leaders are always learning new skills, once perfected; they then teach others what they have learned. Leaders enjoy a sense of accomplishment helping others achieve their goals. Leaders believe their success is dependent on the success of everyone around them.

Leaders live in a "we" world, where the accomplishments of the team are far more important than personal accolades. Leaders are quick to give credit for success to the people they work with.

In contrast, when failures occur, it is the leader who will take responsibility for the blame.

When you're winning it is because of the dog, players, or staff; When you're losing it is because of the trainer, coach, manager

Leaders are always creating an environment which will build confidence of others. Successful people tend to surround themselves with successful people. Hiring the best human person for a job is similar to selecting a puppy, where you look at the dog pedigree and its parent's titles and accomplishments. With humans you also have to look at their pedigree, which are such things as previous employment, accomplishments, awards, titles, training and experience. Knowing how to select the correct person for a specific job skill goes a long way in building a person's success. It also goes a long way to the leader's success. Hiring the correct person for a job makes a leader's job easier; hiring the wrong person disrupts the entire company.

Leaders create environments for people to succeed. Leaders find intrinsic reward in the success in their current or past employees.

Past Behavior Predicts Future Behavior

In contrast, when managers are threatened by the success of subordinates, they limit the opportunities for subordinates. Managers keep secrets from their subordinates and co-workers incorrectly believing if they control information they become indispensable. Managers create barriers; they build walls rather than bridges. Managers are self-centered; they make decisions based on what is in it for them and not their subordinates. Managers have an "I" or me-first mentality. When a failure occurs, managers are quick to point blame at others. Due to their lack of confidence, they are always looking for failures to blame on other people believing such behavior will raise themselves above others. Managers boost their self-esteem by finding and pointing out fault in others.

Great leaders surround themselves with people who possess diverse skill that is highly talented.

Four Stages of Competence

So when you hire a new employee, what do you expect of them on the first day of work? Probably, not much. At the beginning of any new job, before you begin a new class, start a new learning experience, or take up a new hobby, ask yourself how skilled am I at this new endeavor? Your answer is probably not very skilled at this activity. When any of us attempt a new challenge, we are more often than not an unconscious-incompetent.

The four stages of competence is a theory of how we learn initially created by Abraham Maslow. The four step concept was resurrected by Noel Burch in the 1970's as an explanation for the phases of learning.

Unconscious, because we really do not understand how little we don't know. At the onset of any new experience, we do not possess the knowledge to understand how little we know about what we are about to learn or want to learn. We may have a perception or expectation of what we want to learn or expect what the learning will provide us, but this is a belief without experience. A new employee is unconscious when it comes to what the new job involves and what the new employer expects.

Incompetent, because if we do not understand what is expected of us, how can we properly perform the skill? A newly hired individual may have some of the basic technical skills associated with their new job, but not all of the intricacies of the new company's techniques. At this initial stage of learning, a person cannot expect to be anything but incompetent at the required skills of their new job.

For example, when learning to drive a car for the first time, the hand-foot-eye skills needed to accelerate, brake and steer while looking ahead, and checking the rear view and side view mirrors is an awkward and clumsy action at best. Then there is the issue of time and distance needed to accelerate or brake, or the distance to begin a turn. These are just a small sample of many skills needed to drive a car. You cannot learn to drive until you begin to understand what you need to learn.

The first stage of learning is simply an awareness of what the new task will require and becoming conscious of what we need to learn. A novice will most likely have a very different perception of the skills to perform the new job than after mastering the job. Becoming conscious of how much one does not know is a huge step to learning. Realizing what we do not know and what we need to learn, is necessary if any learning is to take place. When this occurs, we have a metamorphosis of the unconscious becoming conscious.

Now we have the Conscious-incompetent. Conscious because the individual is now aware, (possibly only slightly aware, possibly very aware) of what they do not know and what they need to know to become competent. Using the driving example, I now know I need to coordinate my feet, hands, and vision. I recognize some of the physical properties of driving, such as locating the pedals, steering wheel, mirrors, turn signal, shifter, and what they do. But I still do not know how to work each of these physical properties in coordination to move the car.

Such awareness leads to the development of skills and competence, needed to perform the activity we desire to learn. At this point we possess a much better prospective what we need to learn so as to perform the desired activity. When this occurs, we have the transition to the conscious-competent.

A conscious-competent has now acquired the skills to perform a desired job, but must consciously think about each and every component of the desired job before it is properly preformed. At this stage of learning, the individual has to consciously think about every movement and action before it takes place.

Back to the learning to drive example, do you remember when you first learned to drive, to move the car forward you had to consciously think about each and every action you made. First you would think about turning the key in the ignition to start the car, and then think in detail and watch very closely how to push your right foot on the brake pedal, then with meticulous detail, move the shifter to "D" or drive. Now, it was time to think very, very hard about lifting the right foot from the brake to the accelerator while holding tightly to the steering wheel. Each step required very conscious awareness and thinking. The individual has to consciously think about each little step involved in driving.

If the conscious-competent individual practices their newly learned skill, the brain begins to learn patterns called cognitive mapping, otherwise known as habits. Practice, practice, practice lead to the ability to perform an activity without thinking about each little step. Instead, these learned skills have become an unconscious behavior. Yep, you guessed it; the fourth level of learning is the unconscious-competent.

An experience driver (unconscious-competent) is able to get into the driver's seat, place their right foot on the brake, start the car, shift into drive, move their right foot from the brake to the accelerator pedal and not even realize they have performed all of these tasks. The unconscious-competent driver is so practiced at performing this activity they do it without even realizing the many individual steps involved. The unconscious-competent person will drive to work without remembering the ride or the hundreds of decisions made in the process.

At this point, the unconscious-competent is ready to begin building upon this learned behavior and learn a new skill. They are now ready to become an unconscious-incompetent at learning something new.

Food

Operant conditioning is a learning/training technique of shaping behavior most often associated with animal training for aquatic mammals (whales, dolphins, porpoises) at water amusement parks. It has been the basis for most all dog training programs for decades. Food is the principal reward. Operant conditioning is also a very effective training tool with humans, but instead of food, recognition is an effective reward.

Most of us would not go to work if there wasn't a reward involved, known as a pay check. The same concept applies to most everything we do in life; we are looking for a reward. Dogs will work for treats, food, or praise.

Food improves participation and attention.

Food is a powerful motivator in getting animals to respond in a desirable manner. Dogs, horses, dolphins are all trained using food as a reward. Stimulus-response-reward has proven to be the most effective of training techniques, with food as the most effective reward.

Humans will work for money, recognition, praise, and yes, food.

Food is very effective at motivating humans. In Maslow's Hierarchy of need food is a primary physiological motivator, a very fundamental need. People like to eat and when food is provided at education programs, attendance improves. Retention of the information presented at those programs is better when food is provided. Schools which provide student with free breakfasts and lunches attain higher attendance, more participation, and better grades.

Free food is provided by airlines to customers who are experiencing travel complications such as delay or cancelations, because food has a calming effect. When we eat we relax. People become grumpy and complain more when they are hungry. They are much more pleasant when eating or when their hunger has been satisfied.

Food is so powerful it is the most effect technique for controlling prisoner behavior.

The Penitentiaries who served prisoners the worst food have the highest rate of misbehavior. In contrast, prisons with the best menus have the lowest incidence of misconduct. Prisoners with the best conduct are rewarded with better selection of food at their meals compared to those with the worst conduct receiving bread and water. This was found to be the case at Alcatraz Prison; the warden who was most effective at achieving the best prison behavior did so with food. The best behaved inmates received the same food at meals as did the warden and guards. Food as a reward doesn't just work with dogs.

As a sales person I know when I show up to a customer's office with food I get better attendance and more active participation. After achieving a reputation of bringing good food to my in-services; future in-service appointments are a whole lot easier to schedule.

Food is a powerful motivator regardless of the species. Understand when you provide treats to children or co-workers the message you are sending. The activity associated with the food is being reinforced by the food. To humans the reward for work is in the form of a pay check (money). To dogs the reward for a job well done is in the form of food. Food or money represents the same thing; a reward for doing a good job.

When I feed a dog by hand, I then become the alpha dog. The dog now recognizes me as its provider. When, as a sales person, I provide food for a customer, I am now sub-consciously seen as an alpha provider, very powerful unconscious recognition. In animal packs the Alpha is the primary provider of food for the pack members. In human packs, in other words the family unit, the person earning a pay check is referred to as the "bread winner". In animal packs the individual feeding the pack is the perceived leader. The same is true for humans, the person who provides the paycheck is the alpha leader. In humans this is interpreted two ways as both the formal and informal leader.

Whoever in an organization delivers the pay check becomes a perceived leader. If someone from finance department delivers the pay check to your desk every week, then this person gains considerable recognition subconsciously by recipients. Pay check delivery is a valuable opportunity for organization leaders to subconsciously establish in the minds of organization members their leadership position. By personally delivering pay checks and thanking each organizational member for their contribution the person making such deliveries (feeding the pack members) is perceived Alpha. When pay checks are personally delivered with a verbal acknowledgement to each recipient every payday, trust and loyalty follow. Like the Alpha dog feeding the pack the Alpha human feeds (with pay check) the organization members.

As explained earlier in this chapter, it is also important to understand what a dog values as a reward. The more valuable the reward is perceived by the dog, the more motivated the dog is to produce the desired behavior. High valued rewards are used when a new behavior is initiated because it maximizes the dog's attention. After a behavior becomes consistent, then a lesser valued reward can be used to reinforce this behavior.

**You teach people how to treat you
by the way you treat them.**

The way you treat other people is shaping the behavior in which they will treat you. Rewarding humans involves learning how to listen at the correct time or compliment at the correct time, or ask the correct question at the correct time. People who give compliments receive more benefit from the action than do the compliment recipients. People who give compliments have an immediate increase in endorphins providing a feeling of well-being. Rewards can be as simple as thank you, or calling someone by their name, or even just a smile. People like to feel included and their contributions are of value and respected. Recognizing a person's contribution is a reward, which then encourages the recipient to continue similar behavior. People who give honest and sincere rewards build respect with the recipients.

**People do not care how much you know;
Till they know how much you care.**

When shaping human behavior, rewards need to be consistent with the behavior desired. Rewards also need to be consistent with past rewards. How you reward other people with your behavior, whether intentional or unintentional, is what they will repeat. We are always being observed by others, so how you behave is how other people will treat you. Rewards need to take place immediately following a person's desired behavior. If the only time a person receives feedback on their work is at their annual review, the feedback is a waste of time. As a leader, it is important to find people performing desired behavior and reward their behavior as soon as it happens and as often as it happens if you want it to continue.

Reprimands

Reprimands are not effective if this is the only communication with another person. Such behavior is also referred to as nagging, complaining, pestering, hassling, etc. If reprimands are the only feedback a person receives, the recipient will soon block out all feedback. This is what I call becoming a drone. Drones simply do their job going through motions but not working to improve their job or organization.

For a reprimand to be effective it needs to be viewed similar to the removal of a pleasurable experience, in other words the removal of a reward. Rewards are viewed by the recipient as a pleasurable experience. So programing others with frequent positive reinforcement or rewards creates pleasurable expectations. When the pleasure of a reward disappears and is replaced by a reprimand, the reprimand now has a more powerful impact. Rewards or positive reinforcement need to occur at least seven times more often than a reprimand to be effective. Rewards need to be sincere and in response to a specific activity to be effective. The same is true of reprimands they need to be immediate and sincere.

Effective reprimands:
1. Take place in private and not in front of co-workers.
2. Take place immediately following the infraction.
3. Issues are specific to the infraction
4. Explanation or re-training of the correct or desired behavior needs to be provided; see Social Learning Theory.
5. Information is documented in employee file.
6. After the reprimand, move on, do not use the incident as a constant reminder of person's incompetence, move-on.
7. Occur less than once for every seven positive rewards.

It is important to document the reprimand. If the same problem reoccurs you have a record and the issue may have other causes. People fail either because they were not properly trained or because they do not possess the skill to perform the activity.

It is also important to correct undesirable behavior immediately, so this does not become learned behavior. Waiting for the annual review to list all of the mistakes a person has made over the past year is too late to correct past problems. When such a practice is employed the organization has now experienced a years of mistakes which is now learned behavior.

For reprimands to be effective, rewards need to outnumber reprimands at least 7 to 1.

When people get accustomed to rewards, they are very aware when the rewards are removed. Rewards make us feel good and we work to continue receiving them just as the loss of rewards is quickly recognized.

In addition to a formal reprimand to correct unwanted behavior, there are other ways to extinguish undesirable behavior such as withheld listening, or body language indicating disapproval. Shifting recognition and/or listening to another person are also a very effective tool in controlling behavior. Peer pressure is also a very powerful method of controlling behavior. More about these topics will be discussed in future chapters.

If you have to micromanage an employee; you hired the wrong employee.

STEP TO LEARNING

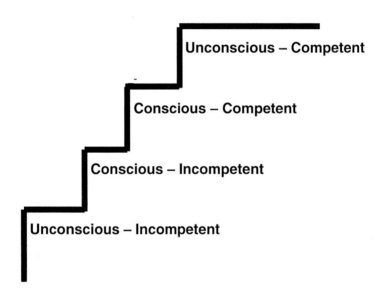

Unconscious – Competent

Conscious – Competent

Conscious – Incompetent

Unconscious – Incompetent

The definition of leadership is

problem solver.

Chapter Four

ZEKE

Bonnie and I were taking a four-day trip to a Pet Supply Store owner's convention in Long Beach, CA. Talk about a weekend of fun!

To most people, taking a four-day trip is a rather simple process. But when you own three Golden Retrievers, taking a trip requires a very large vehicle or finding someone to move into the house to care for the dogs or finding an appropriate boarding kennel. Fortunately, pet supply store clientele provided us with several customers who were breeders and owned boarding kennels.

Bonnie had developed a friendship with one such customer, who was a very well respected Golden Retriever breeder with a beautiful facility. She lived on a large piece of property, in a rural area, with several dog specific buildings, including a fenced-in dog run – all the amenities making owning 16+ Golden Retrievers manageable.

She also had plenty of equipment designed specifically to keep the dog areas clean, while providing them with very nice living and recreation areas. This included individual indoor-outdoor housing kennels for each dog and easy access to a fenced-in, 1-acre piece of property.

The dog run was an acre of fenced property, with a hill in the center. During the day, she allowed the dogs to have the run of this area and by night she would house them in individual kennels in a pole barn-like structure. It was a very safe pleasant area for her Golden Retrievers. The breeder offered each of our dogs their own kennel by night and the opportunity to socialize with her 16 dogs in the fenced-in area by day.

Understand dog breeders keep more females than males for their breeding programs, so of the 16 dogs, 14 were bitches (female dogs) and two were stud dogs. This sounded like and ideal setting to leave our dogs while we were out of town, so we accepted her offer.

On the morning we were to fly out of town, we loaded our three golden retrievers into the back of our SUV and headed for Doggie Camp. Upon arriving, we found her facility to be immaculately clean and beautifully maintained. There was plenty of space for the dogs to exercise and lots of opportunity to socialize.

Our pack consisted of Cindi, an 8-year-old, 50-pound, long legged and short red coat, high energy, svelte, female, field golden retriever. She had a body built for hunting and field work, who had earned a Companion Dog Excellent, (CDX) obedience title. Next was Heidi, a 4-year-old, 55-pound, Golden Retriever, a very soft fluffy strawberry blonde female, with puppy like appearance, who also had earned a CDX obedience title. Last but not least we had Zeke, a 1-year-old, 65-pound, male, Golden Retriever, very handsome, white thick coated, beautifully proportioned to breed standards, with a sleepy eyed appearance. Upon departure from our SUV, they all surveyed the surroundings with a great interest, especially Zeke.

He looked through the chain-link fenced-in exercise area where the owner's dogs were located, and saw 14 female, breeding ages, intact, Golden Retrievers. Within a split second, this sleepy-eyed, slow-moving adolescent male Golden Retriever realized what was in front of him. This had to be a 1-year-old male dog's fantasy of fantasies. His ears perked up, his nostrils flared with the smell of females in the air, and his chest puffed out like Marine at attention. Suddenly, his posture was as tall as John Wayne on his finest day, and he puffed out his coat, making him look like a bodybuilder posing in competition. Even though he was tethered on a leash, Zeke began to strut like a fashion model on a runway. Think of a dog version of walking into a singles bar on a Saturday night. Zeke was showing the girls what a great prospect he was. He was sure every female ("bitches") dog in the fenced in area noticed him as the most attractive dog they had ever laid eyes on. He was trying his hardest to make a favorable impression on those 14 "hot" bitches on the other side of the fence. At this point, Zeke gave me a look which said Thank you! Thank you! Thank you! This is going to be the greatest experience ever.

After a few minutes of greetings and allowing the facility owner a chance to observe how our three dogs responded to the surroundings, it was time for the big moment – entering the exercise area. Cindi and Heidi trotted into the pen socializing with the other girls. They expressed the typical behavior of girls meeting girls at a social event. There were polite greetings, tail wagging, and a lot of friendly gestures toward each other. Zeke, on the other hand, strutted into the exercise area like he was the king of all golden retrievers. As he surveyed his new paradise, Zeke caught sight of a large, extremely handsome, confident, male golden retriever resting on top of the hill.

His name was Falco, and he was an American Kennel Club Grand Champion. He had achieved this distinction in the show ring while being judged by humans. But by his relaxed demeanor, Falco had the respect of all other dogs because of his sheer presence. The other dogs Falco came in contact showed him their respect and you could see he was the Alpha dog of the pack.

Zeke, still standing at the bottom of the hill finally caught sight of Falco at the top of the hill. Falco looked down the hill at Zeke, he didn't stand, nor did he bark, he didn't snarl or show his teeth, he simply looked at Zeke. And, as soon as Zeke caught sight of Falco, he shrunk down like a cut flower, out of water, on a hot day. Poor Zeke, his ears drooped, his shoulders dropped, his chest sank, and he knew, he wasn't the hot stud in town; rather the young pup at the bottom of the pack. The now round shouldered Zeke, with his head hanging down, slowly sulked to a low spot on the periphery of the fenced exercise acre, and assumed his position as the Omega dog, which means bottom of the pack hierarchy.

Dogs quickly assess their social status, in whatever pack they participate. In this case, the position of the pack was well defined by each dog's positon on the hill. Falco was the Alpha male, his position was on the top of the hill, and the next closest dog to Falco was the Alpha bitch of the pack, and so on down the hill till we got to Zeke who was at the lowest and farthest position from Falco.

Dogs know their status in a pack just by the appearance or smell of the other dogs. They do not fight, snarl, bark, bite or have any other altercation to establish pack status, they just simply know. So do humans.

Pack animals know fighting among pack members weakens the pack. They save their energy for hunting to provide food.

SUE

It is Friday afternoon, getting close to quitting time, at a manufacturing company in the middle of summer. Everyone is ready to get out of work and start enjoying the weekend. It is a nice warm day, the sun is shining, and the temperature is perfect for a great weekend of fun. The weather predictions for the next three days show plenty of the same.

As everyone is winding down, the phones in customer service are more quiet than normal. Employees in the manufacturing area are cleaning their work areas. Administration personnel are organizing their desks trying to look busy without starting any projects which could take them past closing time. Then, what no one wants, happens, a call comes in to customer service from a seldom heard customer who is experiencing a product issue which is going to take time to trouble shoot before it can be resolved. The customer service representative answering the call begins to understand the depth of the issue, realizing additional help will be needed to fix the problem. Based on the information the customer service representative receives, this is not going to be a quick, easy fix. In fact, it's going to involve manufacturing, the participation of shipping and receiving as well as the accounting/finance department.

To get this many people involved on a Friday afternoon, who has the power to make these decisions? The customer service rep looks to the leader, who can make things happen. Sue is the manager of customer service, who always seems to get things done. Her first action after getting involved by the customer service rep was to ask questions.

Sue possesses the skill to ask very poignant open ended questions to gather details of the problem. While gathering information, she is documenting what she is learning.

Sue asks the customer representative to keep the customer informed as to what was happening within our organization to solve the customer's problem. Sue makes calls to get Bob from information systems department, then to Tony from manufacturing. Sue explains the issue to both Tony and Bob; they respond to Sue with respect and sincere interest to help, and they both offer suggestions.

At this point, Sue realizes she also needs to contact shipping department and get them involved. Now she has enough information to put together a plan and explains it to all of the informal leaders needed to get the job done, and all the participants respond with true commitment. Sue then gets the original customer service rep involved to explain to the customer how the company will solve the problem. No one is complaining they may have to stay late on a summer Friday afternoon.

Your first impression of this incident may be a customer calling in with a problem is the responsibility of customer service, and the manager has the authority to make such decisions. Which may be true, however this was just one example of a person who always seemed to be the go-to person – whenever there was a crisis? It wasn't because she was the oldest, or because she was the most tenured, or because everyone was scared of her, or even because she was the owner's daughter. Sue was none of those things. Sue had earned the respect of everyone in the company because she had a history of calmly getting things done. Sue had earned the position of customer service manager because of her instinctual leadership. Sue knew how to gather information, who to ask for information, how to make good decisions, how to assign the proper people to the job to get things done, and how to follow up to make sure nothing was missed.

During my years of employment with this company I watched similar events take place and Sue was always the go-to person. Sue was a naturally born alpha. She did not need a big title to earn people's respect. She was a leader and the worker bees knew Sue just quietly and confidently, got things done.

Factotum

Every company I have ever worked for had a Sue, and it usually wasn't the boss or the owner or someone with a big title. These people were the Alpha's of the organization, and most people knew it, in some cases everyone knew it. In fact, in a few cases, the boss/owner even knew it. To be successful in an organization, it is very important to identify the company's Alpha, make friends with them, and learn from them. Webster's term for these people is Factotum's, which means they work outside of their job description for the betterment of the organization. They are the Friday afternoon go to person.

In the case of Sue, when I was hired by the company, she reported to me. After the first several weeks, I realized the respect Sue had throughout the company. I learned she was one of the earliest to show up to work in the morning. So I began arriving at work when she did. I listened and watched her as the people from various departments stopped by her desk and talked to her about problems in their departments. Sue would review the situations with representatives from IT, manufacturing, shipping, billing, etc., regarding issues from earlier in the week. She would review the issues which had not been resolved, inquire about critical customer orders or problems. She was excellent at simplifying situations and formulating answers. The people she met with were not VP's or department heads. They were the informal organization leaders who had earned the respect of other workers; they were without big titles, but they were the people who just simply got things done.

A leader simply makes others better at what they do.

These Alphas' within all companies are people who just simply get things done. So let's get back to the average morning, where Sue, along with a few other employee's, show up for work before anyone else. These are the people who really run the company. It took me a while to figure out how early these folks arrived and who they were, and it was an unlikely group. But I finally figured out when to arrive to listen in on the morning briefings. I would show up in my office about the same time as the informal leaders showed up for work just to learn what was going on. I referred to this morning ritual as "mornings with Sue".

Sue knew I was sitting in my office with the door open listening to the activities at her desk every morning. My next move was to ask if I could participate. With Sue's approval, I became a member of her morning briefings. I pulled up a chair, sat next to her desk with coffee cup in hand and just listened; only interjecting comments when appropriate. I did not try to supersede her leadership within the informal organization structure, rather to learn from it. These morning conversations built rapport with other members of the company and made my job easier. While all of this took place, the formal, titled upper management of the organization were unaware how the organization really functioned.

Pack Behavior

Canines, like humans, are social animals. They like to live in packs, primarily made up of family members. The predecessors to the domestic dog are wild dogs such as wolves, which are very unique. Their primary food source is larger than themselves. An adult wolf weights about 65-70 pounds yet their food source is made up of elk, moose, or buffalo – all of which are over 1,000 pounds each. The food pyramid demonstrates most animals live off of food sources smaller than themselves. For example, bears live on fish such as salmon or forage for berries; fox live on small mammals such as mice or squirrels; Otter feed on shell fish. But wolves are different; they have evolved to feed off large mammals.

Natural Pack

Natural packs are the basic social structure in the human and animal world. A natural pack is most simply defined as a family unit. Members of the same species sharing common family members make up a natural pack. Most wolf packs are family units made up of the parents, mother and father, and the offspring who stay in the pack for purposes of survival. Wolves, unlike most animals, prey on animals larger than themselves, such as buffalo, deer, elk, caribou, and so on. In contrast, bears feed off salmon and whales feed off smaller fish. To feed off animals larger than themselves, wolves must hunt in packs. The pack functions as a well-orchestrated team working together to survive.

Wolves hunt as a pack and identify prey as a group, stalking, chasing, killing and feeding off those animals which make up their food source. Because natural pack members are raised together, they have had their entire lives to develop and understand their hierarchy of leadership. These animals understand the relationship between pack members because they have been raised together. Natural pack members typically spend a lot of time together. They live together, hunt together, eat together, and sleep together.

Wolves live and hunt in a pack in contrast to the other animals, which I have mentioned above hunt as individuals. Because they live and hunt as a pack, wolves are able to feed off much larger prey. It is the team work of the pack which provides the hunting advantage compared to trying to successfully hunt alone. Lone wolves do not survive long in the wild; they need to participate as a pack to have strength.

This is an example of how wolves or dogs are like humans; both are social family or pack animals. A wolf pack is typically made up of an alpha male and female, which usually are the father and mother of other pack members. Offspring usually stay in the pack three years before separating to build their own pack. An average pack of eight wolves works as a family team to find, chase down and feed on large prey. Humans live in family units involving a father, mother, and children. This may also explain how humans and dogs have co-habituated for centuries, each benefiting the other. The unique quality of both dogs and humans, both live in family units working as a team to improve chances of long-term survival. Both canines and humans understand the need for organizational hierarchy of leadership. Without leadership, a group of similar species would simply be in chaos, but with understood leadership, that same group will become a pack, family, or team working together for the good of the whole. Canines do not have elections or assign titles to determine who leads, they simple understand, by behavior, their place in the pack. Humans are no different; they, too, understand who to trust and who to follow.

Artificial Pack

Artificial packs are seldom found in the wild. Artificial packs are made up of strangers who are assembled into teams or work units to achieve a specific goal. Business organizations are artificial packs. The members are not genetically related through family, they are brought together to accomplish a particular goal.

Both natural and artificial packs have a hierarchy of leadership. But the artificial pack has more frequent changes in its membership causing constant changes in the hierarchy structure. This is commonly referred to as company politics. Every time the membership of the pack changes, so, too, does the relationship of its members.

Each change of a packs membership can be easily explained in the organizational chart and reporting structure, they are not so easily defined by the impact it has on individual pack members. Productivity, either positive or negative, is impacted by each change in pack membership.

Sports teams commonly refer to the importance of team chemistry, which is simply the relationship of the members within this artificial pack. Every year, there are stories of sports teams whose season's successes improve or decline after a slight change in the team's players. All it takes is the addition or deletion of one team member to change the group's hierarchy (team chemistry). This, in effect, changes the relationships of everyone on the team, and each member's productivity.

We humans do not recognize most of our lives are spent in artificial packs. We also do not appreciate how the people we meet and work with impact our own behavior. Within every artificial pack, small groups (in high school these are referred to as "cliques") develop. Change just one member of the artificial pack and the members of these cliques change, as do the relationships between the clique's members. In artificial packs, it is the responsibility of the formal organization leadership to create its membership, which indicates the importance of the hiring and firing process is.

Artificial Pack leadership's single most important responsibility is assembling a pack membership effective at achieving the pack's goals. Assembling a successful team is very difficult because it is more than just hiring a desired technical skill. Hiring the best technically skilled individual is important but not if the potential employees core values do not mesh with the established corporate culture. How the new pack member functions within the current pack membership is more important than the degree of technical skills possessed by the individual. Unfortunately, in most cases the interpersonal artificial pack relationships are not understood until weeks after the members have been together. Year in and year out, teams that win the Super Bowl, World Series, Stanley Cup or World Cup are usually made up of pack members who work well together, not necessarily the team possessing the league's most technically talented players. There are stories of a team playing half way through a season, which is playing very mediocre, loses it star player, and suddenly begins winning because overall team performance improves significantly. Or how a player is very average on one team but when traded to another team becomes a major contributor to the team's sudden improvement. One change in pack membership changes the relationships of all pack members. Fitting in with the team culture is integral with individual as well as team success.

The most important decision any leader makes is the hiring of new people to the pack, because each addition or deletion from the pack changes the entire pack dynamics. Whenever a new member is added to the pack; or existing member is removed from the pack the relationships between all of the pack member's changes.

Animal packs are similar to human families the success or failures are a result of the cumulative contribution of all members, via addition or deletion.

The adoption of a puppy to a human family pack is an example of artificial pack. But the younger the puppy is at adoption, such as eight weeks of age, the more closely the puppy will act as a natural member. In contrast, rescuing a dog that has lived in other packs represents an artificial pack.

If the pack or family does not work together their existence will be short term. The same is true of organizations. Without cooperative team work utilizing the unique skills of each member, existence will be short. The strongest and most sustained organizations are those having a well-established foundation.

Formal Organization vs. Informal Organization

Within every artificial organization there is a formal and informal structure. The formal structure is the standard organizational chart with lines and boxes depicting who reports to whom. It has lots of titles to indicate who in the organization has the most power. This is the formal structure the company's boss or owner would like to believe how the organization works. The boss or owner always believes they are the alpha of the organization, but this is less often the case than they realize.

Human beings like to organize everything. They like to put structure to all parts of life, which includes organizational charts of

86

how they believe an organization should work. By assigning tiers and titles, proper chain of command, organizations look so neat, clean and simple. They are nicely organized formal charts, but do not represent the real workings of the organization. Dog packs do not have organizational charts, the pack members know just by watching and smelling who to follow.

A similar example of pack behavior was found on a vacation when Bonnie and I went horseback riding. It is very relaxing to see natural sights up close and personal quietly riding on the back of a horse. Ranches offering visitors with horseback riding excursions usually provide wranglers to supervise the riding experience. The better wranglers are used to having to deal with novice riders and are very good at answering questions. On several occasions, we were paired with wranglers who were entertaining and educational. When such opportunities present themselves, the wrangler serves as a tour guide and the ride becomes a great learning experience. It is from these conversations and observations where I had the opportunity to learn about horse pack behavior. We have been given the opportunity to observe meal time in the corral; the horses would line up to be fed based on their position in the pack hierarchy. The alpha of the herd was first in line followed by the next most respected horse in the herd, then third most respected member of the herd and so on. These positions in the food line were not human imposed; they were completely at the discretion of the members in this herd.

The wrangler explained the feeding hierarchy would remain the same unless a new horse was introduced to the herd or a horse was removed. This is the same behavior we observe in our dog pack as members are added and deleted; each member's position in the pack, from alpha to omega, would change. If we introduced a confident leader to the pack the others would concede to the new leader. In contrast, if we introduced a less confident dog to the pack, others moved up in status.

Within every corporate structure in America, you will find a president or CEO or chairman who, by title, is supposed to be running the business and has the "formal" respect of those who work at the organization. This individual usually occupies a corner office with an exquisite view usually on the top floor of the office building. The vice presidents are then arranged by formal organization title status determined by who has the office closest to the president, the office with the largest square footage of floor space, the next best view compared to the president/CEO/chairman, etc. Directors are then found with lesser views, smaller offices on lower floors than the vice presidents. Next are managers, who occupy even smaller offices with worse views and are located farther from the president/CEO/chairman. This organizational chart is consciously structured to define positions in the organization's social structure.

We think of ourselves, the human beings, as more intelligent and superior to all the rest of the dumb animals on the planet. We have created a very sophisticated pecking order of authority so we can, have buildings constructed with measured office space, and windows to define our status. Reality is humans, as well as dogs, instinctively know the pack structure from alpha down to omega and many times it has nothing to do with the person sitting in the nicest office space.

Informal Organizations

In contrast, every organization also has an informal organization. The informal organization is how, in reality, groups of people actually interact and make the organization function. Titles have no meaning, what is important is who gets things done. People, like dogs, simply understand who they can trust and follow. This is how the informal organization structures functions, members know who to go to when they need help. In your current situation, when you need help, who do you turn to for assistance? This selection is based on past experiences having learned who you can trust and who has shown the ability to get things done.

Using an organizational chart doesn't solve problems. Successful organizations realize the flatter the organization chart, which means the closer the decision maker is to the customer the quicker and easier it is to convert problems to opportunities. Successful organizations have formal leaders who understand hiring the best employees for a particular situation, provide them with the best training to do their job, and trust them to follow through. Organizations that do not create a structure with many layers of management, but rather let the pack establish its own communications for problem solving are very successful. These types of organizations will police themselves attracting high value members and eliminate lesser producing members who are unable to keep up.

The fewer levels of management structure, the more productive the organization becomes, communication is improved and bureaucracy is reduced.

In the human informal organization, verbal communication is often far more accurate and rapid than the formal structure of the organization. By the time a memo is composed, vetted by the proper mangers and properly distributed, the informal organization is already aware of the information. Rumors and gossip around the coffee pot is often more accurate and swifter than any e-mail or memo written by the higher-up.

To illustrate this point, here is an example involving an organization going through rough times they were considering a staff layoff to cut costs. Senior management, in closed secret meetings, was making plans as to how many employees would be involved, who would be involved, when the layoff would occur, how it should be handled, how to explain it to the remaining employees, etc. Every detail of the layoff was being conducted with the utmost secrecy not to alarm any employees.

Three days before the layoff was to occur, Smoky, the man who came into the manufacturing building twice a week to refill the vending machines, (who is not an employee of the organization), said to one of the employees, "sorry to hear you are getting laid-off, I am going to miss seeing you."

The employee responded, "What are you talking about, I don't know about any layoffs." The vending machine employee named additional people who were also being laid off. Three days later, senior management made a "surprise announcement" about a lay off. The names they revealed were the same names Smoky had given days earlier. The informal structure knew as much, if not more, than the formal structure.

The informal organization is a powerful part of all organizations. Knowing how to recognize the informal organization and its leadership is a valuable asset to organizations formal leaders.

Alphas

Alpha dogs are the pack leaders. A natural pack includes both Alpha Male and Alpha Female. The position of Alpha is based on respect from the other members of the pack. Respect is usually the result of age, experience, protection of the pack, care given to pack members, and problem solving skills. Primary responsibility of the Alpha is to keep the pack together and safe. Alphas usually are the lead dog on hunting expeditions to feed the pack. Food, shelter, and pack safety are utmost important to the packs survival. So they are considered the pack member most responsible for feeding the pack as the leader. Leadership is not the result of fear or aggression; it is based on respect and admiration. This can be accomplished through a variety of problem solving behaviors.

It is also interesting; in the dog world the alpha is not always the biggest, strongest or physically imposing member of the pack. The Alpha is the member of the pack with the knowledge to lead and has the trust of the other members to make decisions in their best interest of the entire pack. If any members of the pack change, so, too, does the status structure of each remaining members of the pack including the alpha. In most packs, the alpha hunts, feeds, teaches and protects but does not get into turf battles within the pack. In most organizations we find the same, the true alpha does not get involved in petty turf battles with other organization members. It is the lowest member of a dog pack who is in constant turf battles with other members of similar pack status to determine the omega (lowest member of the pack). In a dog pack, the lowest member of the pack will joust and play fight with one another for social status. You will see the bottom member of the pack bite or grab each another by the nape of the neck. In the human organization, we see the most significant turf wars occurring among the wannabes of organizations, those with unearned formal titles. When one corporate wannabe attacks another corporate wannabe via a personal slam in a meeting or a memo or a comment to coworkers when the other is not around – it is referred to on the human corporate world as "back biting". Interesting how the term explains both the play activity of lower canine animal pack member behavior and the attempts of lesser qualified humans to elevate themselves.

A close look at the social structure of any organization and the relationships within the organization will show how much we, humans, mimic a pack of so-called wild animals. The turf battles for the boss's attention, or more employees, or a bigger office, or a larger budget are usually done between the members of the same organizational level, often in the wannabe level. The front-line employees in an organization do not take part in turf wars; they are too busy getting the work done. It is hard to rock the boat when you are busy paddling. True alphas do not lower themselves to compete in turf wars, arguments, or back biting. Pack members naturally understand who is the most trustworthy to lead. The real contestants in the battle for attention, office size, department space, and formal titles are the wannabes whose justification is based on formal organization titles such as manager, director or vice president. This group will spend their work hours undermining the success of others in attempt to make themselves appear successful. They work for personal gain not in the best interests of the organization.

Leaders vs. Managers

Leadership traits are not learned, they are in our DNA. Leaders are born and not made. In a litter of dog puppies, by 8 weeks of age, the litter has an established alpha, beta, etc. and the entire litter knows and understands where they fit in the litter hierarchy. These are 8 weeks old or younger puppies understanding by instinct who to follow. The members of the litter do not take a vote, or have assigned titles; it is learned by their interaction with each other. Humans, like dogs, are born into their hierarchical status. By 7 years of age most humans have 97 percent of their values in place, and among other humans of the same age, recognize the hierarchy structure.

People like dogs, look for leaders within whatever pack they participate. Without political elections or assigning formal titles, people recognize who in the pack is the best leader. In fact, all species in their own way recognize who in the pack is the best leader. A good leader typically is a good provider of food and shelter. They are good teachers. They organize the pack. They work on the best behalf of the entire pack, not for individual benefits. A pack is structured in a hierarchy with the leader designated as the alpha, based on their contributions to the pack, remaining members assume the remaining roles or positions as beta, gamma ... omega.

In a human pack the most important responsibility of a leader is surrounding one's self with the best people for each job, in other words, putting the right people in the right place to do the right things. Knowing how to hire is the most important talent a human business leader can possess. Hiring the correct people separates great teams from average teams. Hiring the wrong people can destroy an organization.

After hiring the best people, leaders provide their pack with the appropriate training for each position. This is where each person is taught the best skills to perform their job. Training is critical to preparing pack members how to do their job.

Next successful leaders need to equip their staff with the appropriate tools to do their job at the highest level. Sometimes this means creating new tools for specific jobs. That is part of the creativity of leadership, finding new tools to help their pack achieve success

When a leader has the right people, properly trained, and equipped to do their job, it is time to get out of their way. Let them do their jobs. Trust them.

At this point a leader becomes a coach, paying close attention to their packs progress without interfering. Through observation and asking questions, the leader insures the pack members are working together and heading in the correct direction. Making sure everyone knows their job and doing it properly. When needed, a leader will make the appropriate adjustments using rewards and reprimands.

The fifth skill of a leader is to know when things are not going correctly and changes need to be made. Leaders recognize when a person is not producing the desired results. They understanding how to best correct the situation, either by more training, changing job responsibilities or separation.

In contrast managers are a creation of formal organizations. They are provided a formal title intended to establish respect, expecting other organizational members will then follow. Managers are put in place to follow orders. They are responsible for carrying out the plans of leadership. The word manager has become overused in a very generic non-descript title. Here are some of the manager titles I have recently seen (these are real titles from real organizations): New Product Ingredient Junior Account Manager; Customer Experience Manager; Outbound Telemarketing Sales Account Training Manager; Aftermath Sales Manager; or Infrastructure Solutions Field Manager Trainee. The title manager has become a word to either impress the person who possess it or confuse everyone else.

The dictionary definition of manager is somebody who is responsible for directing and controlling the work and staff of a business or of a department within it. In contrast a leader is defined as somebody who guides or directs others.

In this book I will use the word leader as someone pack members instinctually look to for a vision, including goals and plans, which they respectfully cooperate and embrace. A manager is pack member given a formal title, following specific guidelines to achieve a technical goal.

Things to Remember

A leader is a natural problem-solver.

A leader is someone who can look at chaos and find clarity.

A leader evaluates the opportunities and obstacles.

A leader draws from experience and knowledge to determine the most useful assets for a given situation.

A leader assembles the most appropriate tools.

A leader develops a plan or creates a vision.

A leader communicates the plan/vision to enlist support.

A leader teaches and trains the needed skills.

A leader produces a feedback system and utilizes the feedback to adapt, adjust and fine tune.

Managers do the right things, leaders do thing right.

Peter Drucker
Economist

"Anything the mind can conceive and believe, the body will achieve."

Napoleon Hill

Chapter Five

Liz

Responding to a telephone call from a concerned neighbor, the local humane society found a boney, very thin, red coated golden retriever chained to a post behind a vacant house. The abandoned house was located in a neighborhood close to a college. The school year ended and summer vacation for the students had begun.

The dog was skin and bones, dehydrated and malnourished with a very thin coat. There was no hair on her neck or underbelly from the constant rubbing of her chain collar and tether, which had been tearing out her fur while she tried to free herself. The chain was usually running from the collar down between her front legs then her rear legs dragging across the ground to the stake in the ground where is was attached.

Since she had to run tethered to a post by a chain she was constantly maneuvering her legs so they were able to move around the chain. Her front legs moved in a more circular than a normal front to back gait. Though thirsty, hungry, and abandoned, the dog greeted Humane Society workers with excitement and a wagging tail. She was thrilled to get attention – any attention - from anyone. Within a short time, the Humane Society workers realized they had a very high energy dog on their hands. This dog was supercharged, which did not make her the most attractive dog for most people looking to adopt a pet.

She was rather overwhelming with a great deal of zest, frightening away prospective adopters. Her high level of energy and constant quest for trouble was probably the cause of her getting chained to a post in the yard. Her undesirable behavior made it clear to the folks at the Humane Society this stray was probably not adoptable. Her appearance didn't help either since she lacked hair around her neck and underbelly.

At the time, my wife, Bonnie, was on the board of directors for this Humane Society and during a board meeting at the shelter the executive director, knowing Bonnie owned and loved golden retrievers, told her about this high strung, wild, golden retriever whose life expectancy was running very short. Before leaving, Bonnie visited the crazy red head finding all the stories to be correct. She encountered a bony, thin coated, over energized, leggy bitch. In very short order, I too, was visiting the terrorist at the shelter. Only this visit resulted in an immediate adoption.

Having been a stray, the red-headed golden retriever escape artist came without a name, so when we adopted her, we named her Liz. Just because the environment changed when she moved into our house, Liz's previous learned behavior did not. When she moved in with us her earlier life experiences (programming) taught her to receive attention, required negative behavior. This is where I learned if a dog is not stimulated and challenged to learn desired behavior, they will take it upon themselves to find their own stimulation.

This is also where the fun began. The first things we learned about this dog, she was very smart and had perfected the art of slipping out of any collar around her neck or any restrictive devise related to a leash. Like Houdini in a locked trunk, a collar, on her, would not stay on her neck very long. She could slip her head out of a collar faster than her human handlers could react. When she would get loose, she delighted in playing the game of "catch-me-if-you-can".

This dog could run! She loved to run. What she really loved more, was having someone chase her. This was the ultimate running experience. She was not going to be caught until it was her decision to come home. Her escapism did not just apply to collars, either. It also included any house door with access to the outside. If the door was not securely closed, she would unlock a latch, push her way out and she was gone. What she learned in the first six months of life was the quickest way to get attention was to do something wrong because attention quickly followed.

Whenever Liz was not the center of attention, she would steal a hair brush or a tube of toothpaste from a bathroom drawer or socks from a clothes drawer or food off the kitchen counter. Yes, she could open drawers. She had no sense of correct animal behavior nor had ever been taught boundaries. She had the athleticism and coordination to jump, landing all four legs on top of a kitchen counter. Since this is where food was kept, it just seemed like the natural thing to do, so she did.

The first task was to change this dog's behavior from a loner trying to survive into a functional pack member. We needed to reprogram her thought process from deviant behavior to positive desirable behavior. I thought the best first step should be teaching her to walk on a leash. But as soon as she was attached to a collar and leash, she would thrash and fight like a trophy game fish being reeled in. Her constant fighting and thrashing gave me the feeling of holding on to a bucking bronco. While at the same time she worked very hard to slip her collar and free herself from this restrictive leash to begin a game of catch me if you can.

After finding a wide variety of collars that Liz could slip, we found she was unable to slip a pinch collar, which looks like an instrument of torture but when used properly it does not choke nor does it inflict pain, but most importantly, it would not slip off. The first lesson was to get her to stop thrashing fighting the lead and just walk. Every time she would calm down and walk even for the shortest distance – two or three steps – I would praise her as lavishly as if she had just won the Westminster Dog Show and quickly followed giving her dog treats. Her calm behavior only lasted a few steps, then as though she had been jolted with an electric charged cattle prod, the crazed fighting for freedom resumed. These walks were far more fatiguing to my arm than to my legs.

Did I mention Liz had abundant energy which never seemed to subside?

When not under direct adult supervision, this little redhead had to be locked in a dog crate because in addition to being an escape artist, she was also very destructive. Liz was a master of chewing, clawing, and climbing on anything breakable. She was a one dog demolition crew.

After several weeks, what we observed, following a good run or an extended time on her feet, Liz was limping on her right front paw, which pointed outward to the right like a ballerina in first position. Initially, it was not easy to distinguish the limp due to her already bow-legged gait developed during her months maneuvering around the tethering chain between her legs.

After explaining the problem to our local vet, he recommended we take Liz to an orthopedic specialist associated veterinary clinic at the state university about 90 miles from our house. On the first visit, the vets conducted multiple x-rays and tests. Based on their findings, the problem was diagnosed as a torn rotator cuff.

During the orthopedic surgeon's manual examination including turning and rotating her right front leg and shoulder, while at the same time he was looking at the X-Rays, Liz sat stoically staring at him. The veterinarian commented she is a very, very tough dog, based on his experience with such injuries and what the X-rays showed, she should be howling in pain.

That was Liz – a very, very, tough dog.

Surgery was scheduled for Monday morning and the surgeon wanted Liz dropped off at the clinic on Sunday night. He explained, if all went well we could visit Liz on Tuesday and she could possibly go home as soon as Friday or Saturday. The surgeon said he would not let her go home until she was able to walk on the repaired leg. So my plan was to drive to the university veterinary clinic, located about 90 miles from our house and visit Liz after work Tuesday night.

On Monday we received several phone calls from the University Veterinarian clinic staff, first telling us the surgery was a success. The next call was from the surgeon giving more details of the procedure. The third call was to let us know Liz was coming out of the anesthetic. All good news.

At 6 a.m. on Tuesday, we received a phone call from the orthopedic surgeon. Oh no! What could have happened? No one calls this early in the morning with good news. As I answered the phone, thinking the worst, the surgeon began the conversation, how soon can you pick up your dog?

Is she dead? Which was my first reaction? The surgeon's response was no, she is doing just fine, but you can pick her up immediately!

Immediately? I reacted, what happened to your original statement 'if all goes well she can go home on Friday or Saturday? I explained both Bonnie and I had to work all day but I could pick up Liz after work. He kept insisting the sooner the better and Liz was ready to go home. After work, I drove to the University Clinic to bring Liz home. I entered the building after 7 p.m. It was after-hours; the clinic was dimly lit and deserted. No one was working at the reception desk so I walked through the building looking someone who could help me. I was approached by a young veterinary resident; I explained who I was and the dog I came to pick up. The resident's eyes got really big, and then he turned and quickly scurried down a hallway loudly exclaiming "the man for the devil dog is here."

In a very short time, the veterinary resident returned, followed by a group of co-workers, holding on to a taunt lead with Liz slipping and sliding on the freshly waxed tile floor while pulling him down the hall. When she arrived two days ago for surgery she was boney with very little hair, but now she had about 25 percent of her body shaved for the surgery and an incision stretching from just below her neck to below her rib cage. She was quite a homely sight. But, the surgeon was correct; she could walk on the surgically corrected leg. Liz jumped on me, with her front legs on my chest, while her rear legs spastically slipping and sliding on the waxed tile floor.

The residents, as a group, quickly explained I was to keep her quiet and not stress the incision or repaired shoulder. The veterinary residents gave me some antibiotics and waved goodbye. I was not in as big a hurry to leave as they wanted me to be. How can I keep her quiet? Can you give me some tranquilizers? No, we do not believe in tranquilizers, the pain and discomfort should keep her quiet. Uhhh, it doesn't seem to be working now!

The residents assured me we would be fine and in unison waved good bye. I was still very curious why the change in plans from Friday or Saturday to immediately and was not going to leave without more information. This is when I learned that in the space of 48 hours, Liz had tipped over the dog crates, surgical trays, IV's and a variety of other items when she was supposed to be recovering. She also got loose and caused a variety of other damages to the clinic. The drive home was not much better. I had her kenneled in a dog crate in the back of my SUV. The crate was rocking and rolling and bouncing around the entire trip home.

The rotator cuff surgery was performed successfully, repairing her damaged right shoulder. For Bonnie and me, the surgery was the easy part; it was the recovery and rehab, which was long and challenging. It was difficult trying to control this over energized crazy golden retriever, who wanted to run and play. She did not recognize pain nor did she understand there was a huge incision, extending from her neck to her ribs filled with many stitches, which needed quiet time to heal. As well as the bones, muscles and ligament which had been surgically repaired also needed quiet time to heal. I believe Liz's recovery took more out of Bonnie and me than it did Liz. Fortunately, our local vet had spent enough time with Liz to understand she was not about to peacefully lay around the house allowing her shoulder and incision to heal, so Liz was put on a strong dose of sleeping pills. I emphasize, a strong dose, because it took a lot of medication to keep her quiet.

It took several months, of heavy medication, before Liz had healed enough to begin rehab and resume her normal devious activities of slipping collars and breaking out of secured house doors.

Liz was not a pretty example of a Golden Retriever. She was leggy, long bodied, and rather disproportionate in shape and structure. Even after her shoulder surgery, she ran with legs going in every direction. When she ran it looked like she had six legs. With all of that said, she could out run or out swim just about any other dog she ever played with. And despite all of these shortcomings, Liz wasn't afraid of anything.

Not only was she stoic to physical pain, she was emotionally hardened. Liz had learned in her short life the only thing she could depend on was herself. Liz did not trust anyone. Nor did she believe anyone would take care of her.

We could not continue living defensively with a dog who was always thinking of ways to get loose and when successful we had to react and respond to the escapee's exploits. So, basic obedience was needed. But this was easier said than done. After the first class at several different dog training schools, we were given our enrollment money back and asked not to return to class. This is where we needed to look beyond the usual basic dog obedience training of pop the leash, and then jerk the dog around to get a desired response. Liz had proven she was oblivious to pain.

So, I took a lesson from my Master's Degree in Organizational Behavior of trying to find what motivated this dog. Thus began evening training in the basement. We had a semi-finished basement with several small rooms with solid, but unfinished, walls and a concrete floor. I would lock Liz and myself in one of these small basement rooms for about an hour every evening feeding her dinner. The first several nights consisted of me holding food in my hand in an attempt to build her trust such that she would willingly approach me. But Liz was far more interested in inspecting the layout of the room – looking for a way to escape.

She inspected the perimeter walls looking for any crack or opening that would allow her body to slip through. It took several days to get the first breakthrough, Liz calming down enough to stop planning her get away and walk to me to take food from my hand. This was a huge step for her, a display of trust. It may sound very simple but it was a big emotional leap for her. For the next several nights all I asked of her, was to just trust me to feed her.

My next step was to move to different locations in the room trying to get her to take food treats from my hand. I was trying to build on her initial trust to seek me out for food. Small steps, small progress, separated by large intervals of time. After Liz responded with a desired response, she received food treats accompanied by words of praise. She still did not trust me enough to let me bend over and pet her as a reward. Liz still did not have the confidence my touching her would not result in something bad happening.

When I would lean toward her to provide a physical reward she would skirt away. We continued nightly training in isolation, void of distractions. Slowly she began to associate food reward with the verbal commands, come, sit, stay, down, heel. Each of these commands took days to produce a desired result. Every correct response by Liz resulted in her receiving food treats, her dinner, kibble by kibble. Once Liz learned to sit, then we worked on sit in heel position (heel position means the dog sit at the handlers left side, both facing the same direction) then it was time to take a step and get her to follow my lead staying in heel position. Once she learned to follow me for one step forward, treat, then it was one step to the right, treat. Her trust and confidence was building, so next I would take one step backward and she would follow.

It was at about this point she would accept physical touches of praise. We had gotten to the point Liz, found verbal and physical praise more important than food. I learned once we got past her wall of distrust for me (or for that matter, anyone), what Liz wanted more than anything, was recognition, either verbal or physical. My words of praise were important, but of even greater impact was the tone and inflection. Bending over to pet her was of greater value to her than any food reward. It got to the point where I used very little food when training, but instead fed Liz a healthy diet of verbal and physical praise. Liz responded with greater interest when receiving praise than when receiving food rewards.

**If a dog does not receive recognition for positive behavior;
it will create negative behavior for recognition**

The relationship built between Liz and I seemed to calm her down and reduce some of her destructive behavior. At this point, her obsession to escape from our house and run was not as strong as it had been. She still had destructive episodes, but they were occurring less often. Sometimes she would jump on to the kitchen counter, cruise the counter surface eating what smelled good while pushing less desirable items off the counter onto the floor.

Other times, we would take her out to go potty for 20 minutes and she would do nothing, then come back inside the house head to the middle of the living room look us directly in the eye, then squat and poop. These were behaviors she had learned early in life guaranteed to solicit a reaction from humans. She did not know right from wrong or good from bad – what she did know was how to get a reaction out of the humans rewarding her bad behavior with recognition. When Liz was bad early in our relationship, I reacted with a normal response, quickly reprimanding her then discharging her to a dog crate. She had learned in the first nine months of her life the only way to receive recognition was to do something "bad" getting humans to react and provide her with an intense level of recognition.

But, after my basement isolation training experience with Liz, the new response to her bad behavior was to act as if she was "non-existent." Whenever she did something bad, we would not acknowledge it or her for several hours. The longer she was not given attention, the quieter she became, and the farther she retreated.

But, when Liz did anything desirable she now received exaggerated praise. Even the smallest positive behavior was reason to throw her a party. It was important to produce repeated desired behavior by repeatedly rewarding the desired behavior, while ignoring undesired behavior. It did not take many of these "non-existent experiences" before Liz stopped her non-desired behavior. Liz discovered rewards for desired behavior was more pleasurable than being non-existent. She had been reprogramed, learning what appropriate behaviors would elicit the reaction she wanted.

Praise needs to outnumber reprimands; at least 7 to 1, for a reprimand to be effective.

After she understood how performing desired behavior resulted in rewards, recognition, and respect, her learning progressed at an exponential rate. She loved attention. It wasn't until we entered an obedience dog show which I began to realize how powerful her drive was for attention.

Obedience dog competition is where a dog and human work as a team performing a variety of exercises while being scored by a judge who is also in the show ring. There are several exercises for each level of competition, for example at the lowest level of competition, novice, the dog-handler team are required to heel on and off leash, following a judge's verbal direction.

You have to give respect before you will earn respect

It was during dog show competition I gained even more respect for Liz. She was a good dog to train, not great, just good. When we practiced, she could do the exercises, not very sharp or crisply, but she understood how to perform the components of each exercise. So, when I entered my first obedience trial with Liz, I did not have high expectations. That was until we walked into the dog show ring, suddenly she became a star. Liz walked into the show ring; sure everyone attending this event was there exclusively, to see her, and only her. Her posture became more erect, her eyes became wider and brighter, she walked with a lilt in her step. There was a purposeful exactness to everything she did. Liz loved going to shows because she received attention.

When we practiced and trained, she would receive treats as incentive and reward, but food is not allowed in a show ring. Yet when we were at dog shows competing, she sensed the competition and the audience and she enjoyed it far more than any food. Many people and/or dogs do not handle stress well and actually self-destruct when in competitive situations. There are others who thrive on competition and stress; they perform better when in a stressful situation than in a normal environment. Liz thrived under this kind of stress.

Many of the most acclaimed Broadway actors need an audience to produce a great performance. The same is said about the greatest athletes, who perform their most brilliant athletic feats at the biggest events. No stage is too big for this group of people. Liz treated dog shows as her personal stage.

Before I began working with her in obedience and showing her, Liz was slipping collars, unlatching doors to free herself and run. Our first Novice trial was held outside in a community park; Liz was heeling next to me, off leash, with far more interest in following my instructions than running free. She could have run off in any direction at will. But the recognition and praise was far more attractive. So much so, she took first place not only that day but also the next two shows which were also outdoors.

Liz was a confident dog. She was born with confidence. If she hadn't been so confident she probably would not have survived her first year of life. She loved receiving recognition, so if following training commands resulted in receiving recognition this became far more fun than getting into trouble.

At this point, I believe respect was established between Liz and me. She craved praise, so training was easy, if recognition was involved she wanted to learn and please. We quickly earned a variety of obedience, rally and agility titles from a variety of major canine sanctioning organizations. I believe Liz, somehow understood if she learned new exercises she would continue to travel to all those really neat places where people would show up, just to see her perform. And her confidence rubbed off on me. The more excited she would get to show, the more fun I was having, which further encouraged me to enter more trials, train new exercises, learn new training techniques.

Winning is fun and contagious.

Success builds confidence, which is how sports teams have winning streaks; confident teams go into games knowing they will win, not hoping they will win. Confident people are excited about competition. Confident people like to learn new things. Scared people avoid competition, worry more about what they have to loose than how much they can prosper.

Until Liz arrived in my life, I'd never had any interest in devoting the time and work required to compete in the higher levels of dog obedience, rally and agility classes. But because she enjoyed learning and training so much, it was the first time I ever had any interest in pursuing such titles. These are the behaviors of people who are having fun and enjoy learning. The eight years with Liz taught me more than any other experience in my life.

DELIVERY TECHS

My first sales management job was working for a company providing home health equipment for patients. These services were provided through a network of locally based offices spread across a three-state area. The ten sales reps reporting to me were assigned geographic territories each with multiple community-based delivery offices. I was hired because the company had experienced frequent turnover in virtually all positions, which was cause for the declining sales and profits.

My initial meetings with the sales people took place on an individual basis at one of the offices in their territory. I found a consistent pattern with each office I visited – morale was low, turnover was high.

A local office typically employed a manager; an allied health care professional, such as a home health nurse or respiratory therapist; customer service telephone representatives, and delivery techs. The majority of employees, in these offices were delivery techs. The delivery techs drove trucks, stocked with products such as oxygen, home health care equipment, walkers, wheelchairs, hospital beds, commodes, etc. for that days patient's home deliveries.

The most profitable product was home oxygen, which was delivered as compressed gas in large metal cylinders, or frozen in liquefied form within giant metal thermos containers, or oxygen concentrators. All of these people were hourly employees with minimal skills and training for their job. Due to the method of product delivery and patient services, the delivery techs had the greatest interface with customers. Most were lacking in confidence. They were distrustful of management, had negative attitudes and for the most part just trying to get through the day to earn a pay check.

On my initial visits to these locations, I found a great deal of distrust toward me. People avoided talking with me, trying to get as far from me as possible. It took a lot of coaxing to have a conversation with anyone, even the sales people. Due to the high turnover of staff in all positions, everyone was cautious of anyone new. My past experiences had taught me more can be learned by listening than talking, so on my field office visits I did more observing of office functions than providing any directives. Most of the office conversation consisted of complainants, negative comments and sarcasm. Staff seemed to feed off each other's negativism. This is an example of learned behavior of negativism as the staff at these remote local offices verbally rewarding each other for berating the company they worked.

Seagull Management

The only time these remote patient care locations received any communication with upper management or the corporate office was a reprimand of some sort, they had developed a very negative opinion of management. Communication with management most often took place via phone; seldom did anyone with a management title visit these outreach locations. On special occations someone with a management title would fly into meet with employees, tells them all of the things they are doing wrong, defecates on their ideas and activities, then fly's out, departing as quickly as they arrived. This type of behavior is referred to as Seagull Management.

However, there was one topic virtually all the staff would talk about using kind and compassionate words, the patients they served. They loved the patients they took care of. Armed with this knowledge, I had a starting point. I got them to talk about their patients. Once I could get the staff to begin talking about the patients they cared for, frowns and disgruntled attitudes turned to empathy, compassion, and brighter facial expressions. They told me how many of their customers provided coffee, cookies, or other treats while these employees made their deliveries, but the real rewards the employees received from their jobs were the intrinsic good feelings coming from helping someone in need.

I tried to schedule days to ride with delivery techs to better understand their jobs. One of the things I learned was they did not carry any business cards or anything to leave behind with the patient, which would have our the delivery techs name, company name, phone number, office contact person other than what was on the delivery form.

Most days consisted of the office manager, who might also be the office allied health care provider (nurse or respiratory therapist) or customer service staff creating a delivery route for each of the delivery techs. Each product delivery had a time allotment for delivery used to help plan the day.

My job responsibilities were to increase sales with understaffed, geographically-stretched sales teams, who were working in offices alongside undercompensated, frustrated staff. Financially, the company could not justify more sales people; so how could we maximize the effectiveness of these sales people with huge territories to cover?

I learned all of the employees were minimally trained in their job responsibilities, including equipment options and services the company provided. Very few of them understood the information required on each delivery form.

My first step was to train the sales reps on the services and equipment the company provided. Every day, each sales rep was to provide me with a brief, easy to understand explanation of just one product or service we offered. After each sales representative felt comfortable with the materials doing for several weeks, I then asked each of them to provide the same training to the offices in their territory. I asked if they would have a 15-minute staff meeting every morning in the office they were working that day to review just one piece of equipment or service we provided. The meeting included an easy to read "cheat sheet" of quick and easy reference information the staff could use to answer questions.

Initially, these meetings were met with resistance. It was not an easy sell. I had to stimulate attendance by providing food. If a staff member was identified as knowledgeable on a particular product or service they were asked in advance to be a key member of the presentation. As often as possible, we would employ the knowledge of our manufacturer's sales people to explain the products we carried. Only after persistently encouraging the sales people to make these training sessions an all the time program did the staffs begin to recognize the benefits. In time, these programs became well received, especially by the delivery techs; they wanted to know more about their job. This is where it really became fun.

The next step was to teach the staff about the medical conditions their patients were experiencing such as explaining the physiologic effect each disease would display. This helped to explain what the delivery form letters represented, such as COPD for Chronic Obstructive Pulmonary Disease or MD for Muscular Dystrophy or LC for Lung Cancer or MS for Multiple Sclerosis and what signs and symptoms a patient with each disease would display. By teaching the staff the debilitating effects of each disease they could better understand the importance of the equipment delivered. At this time we created reference sheets for each of these diseases listing the home health care product commonly used by these patients and why it was useful.

Delivery techs were the employees from our company who saw the patient's living conditions, such as if it was a one- or two-story house, where bath rooms were located, the need for any other aids to daily living. But without the knowledge of what services and equipment we provided, the physically visit the patient's environment had no meaning. After the techs acquired knowledge of equipment and services, they could make recommendations making their patient's lives easier. Such recommendations were communicated by the tech to customer service, who could order and bill for such services.

Next, I introduced morning case studies, similar to what physicians do during grand rounds, which included an explanation of a patient's disease, a description of the person's living conditions and what our company could do to make the patient's life easier. The delivery techs became the morning meeting leaders, and they talked about a patient to whom they provided service, the patient's disease, their living condition, the equipment used, and what could be done to improve the situation. This is where the delivery tech begins receiving the respect of others for their knowledge. This was very powerful. What started out months earlier as 15-minute meetings which staff did not want to attend, evolved into 45-60 minute daily, start-the-day sessions with nearly 100-percent attendance. Staff members were even arriving early for work to prepare their portion of the days learning sessions.

The meetings had become an intrinsic reward experience which not only built company knowledge but also self-esteem. These meetings turned into an opportunity for applause, high-fives, smiles, laughter, and a sense of team. Based on what staff members learned from each other they began turning to each other for help and information.

Respect gets respect

Several weeks into the program, I had business cards printed for everyone in every office. This may sound like a very simple item, but it created a huge personal internal positive reaction. This is called recognition. I was told many times how proud they were to show the business cards, with their name printed, to family and friends. Yes, the add-on sales as a result of the recommendations made by delivery techs generated a big difference in sales. With the growth in sales, I was able to provide better morning meeting treats, which also seems small but was another powerful reward.

 Other interesting changes I observed during this process was how the personal appearance of staff improved. The general cleanliness and appearance of the offices improved, people took greater respect in themselves and it was reflected in the way they appeared and treated others. People like to learn. We like to help others. We all want to be recognized as someone of value for what we have to offer.

This is another example of how one person's behavior controls the behavior of others. When I found an employee neatly dressed and groomed I was quick to recognize it with a compliment. Such recognition was not just for the recipient, but for other employees within ear shot who also wanted recognition, and in time other staff members would also improve their appearance.

I would try to find somebody at the meeting doing something right, any desired behavior, as tiny and insignificant as it might be, was worthy of recognition. Recognition can come in a small simple statement as "good job", "I like the way you do...", and "nicely done". Recognition, like a smile, is contagious. It takes time, but sooner or later, those who have received recognition will start looking to find others doing something desired and provide some form of recognition as well. Simple little things such as thanks, I appreciate your help, thanks for your help, etc., and others in the office picked up on what was happening.

Compliments are contagious

When a person gives another person a compliment, the person giving the compliment receives a boost of oxytocin which is a blood born endorphin, producing a feeling of happiness. So giving compliments is a self-induced dose of happiness. Which means the compliment giver enjoys more positive feelings than does the recipient. It is a win-win situation because the recipient also benefits from the compliment.

Solitary confinement is the severest form of punishment.

After several months of training Liz, I was reminded of information I had learned years earlier regarding punishment. Based on articles I had read about prisoners of war (POW's) and convicts, they reported the harshest form of punishment is solitary confinement. I had read people who had experienced solitary confinement for extended periods of time, said they would have preferred a physical beating over prolonged periods of isolation.

In a very simple test of pain and isolation, students at the University of Virginia were used to better understand isolation. Selected students were placed in a chair in a sterile white lab room and told to sit and do nothing. The room and everything in it was white, sound proof, had no windows, and was devoid of stimulation. Infrequently, the subjects were given an electric shock. After several electric shock experiences the subjects were asked to rate the pain. They were then asked would you pay to avoid this pain, the unanimous answer was "yes".

At a later date, the subjects were asked to return to the sterile white lab room with no form of entertainment and told to sit quietly with a hand-held push button device they were told if depressed would administer an electric shock similar to what they had experienced in the previous session. This time, the infliction of pain was self-imposed. It was up to the individual to shock themselves. After a short time of being subjected to stimulation free solitary confinement, virtually all of the subjects shocked themselves because of boredom. People would rather endure pain than be secluded in isolation.

In the 1950's, in South America primitive tribes were found by explorers who had spent their entire existence undetected by the outside world. They had been isolated from other societies, thus maintained their own form of government, rule and punishment. These people had established norms and morals for tribal members to follow. Breaking of their tribal laws resulted in penalties. Breaking the most coveted laws of the tribe resulted in the offender being considered a non-person. Tribal law mandated a non-person was to be totally ignored by the other tribe members. For all intents and purposes, the non-person ceased to exist in the eyes and ears of the other tribe's people. After a period of time the non-person believed themselves they did not exist. Taking away the ability to interact with other

116

members of the non-person's community ultimately resulted in the non-person wandering off into the brush to commit suicide.

Complete withholding of all interpersonal interaction is actually capital punishment in the most torturous manner. Putting people in isolation is severe punishment. Communication is a critical element toward developing trust and involvement.

Dogs are like humans, they are social animals. Both humans and dogs are at their best when they live and work in family packs. Separation from interaction with others is painful. Such separation at an early age can lead to distrust and fear of others.

After my basement training with Liz, I believe she had been left tied up alone in the back yard of the house for hours, days, and without human interaction. She found misbehavior was rewarded by the appearance of a human breaking her term of isolation with a severe physical reprimand. Similar to the humans who experienced solitary confinement, a physical beating was better than isolation. By the time we adopted Liz, she had been programed with isolation followed by physical abuse was to her understanding normal behavior.

Let's go back to the evening basement training sessions. It took several months and a multitude of very small steps, before Liz would take verbal commands and respond with the appropriate behavior. At this point, she responded stronger to praise than to food rewards. I now had more influence over Liz's behavior with the tone of my voice and its inflection, than any collar, leash, or harsh punishment. Her early learning experiences taught her punishment was desirable. She had developed a very high tolerance for pain so physical punishment was not an effective method to change behavior. It was during the basement re-programing of her behavior where she figured out the recognition she so craved could be accomplished by following a human's requests.

When you are winning it is the dog, and when you are losing it is the handler.

This is a term used at dog shows pointing out the impact the handler has on the behavior of their teammate, the dog. The dog's performance in the ring is based on the handler's training leading up to the dog show performance and the handler's commands and leadership during the dog show performance. If the dog makes an error during the dog show performance, 99.9 percent of the time it is because of the way the handler trained the dog to perform a part of an exercise. Or, the handler, due to nerves, made a mistake in the ring and gave the dog wrong information. The same can be said for any team or organizations performance. When you are winning, it is because of the player or employee, when you are losing it is because of the coach, manager, or boss.

Teams and organizations take on the persona of their leadership. Teams and organizations which are led by people skilled at hiring and training, tend to produce successful outcomes. Every year, I hear these same comments about the coaches and managers of top performing professional and amateur sports teams, they are great teachers, and they are always teaching.

Lordstown Syndrome

People like to be recognized for their work and when they do not get recognition for productive behavior, they begin to find ways of getting recognition for negative behavior. When I was working on my Master's Degree, I read a story about a man who noticed a rattle in his recently purchased new 1970 automobile. When he took the car back to the purchasing dealership the service department was unable to identify the source of the rattle.

The mechanic who worked on the vehicle went through the usual list of items to check and tighten and adjust and sent the customer off with the impression the problem had been repaired. But in a short time, the rattle continued and the owner returned to the dealership service center with the same complaint. Once again, the mechanic went through the check list of common causes and places for a rattle adjusting and tightening each. The customer was sent home with the assurance the rattle was gone. It wasn't and the customer returned to the same dealership service center again and the pattern continued.

After numerous return visits, the now very angry customer took his complaint to the owner of the dealership who then loaded members of the dealership into the car to let them hear the noise. They all heard the noise, but could not recognize exactly what was causing it. So, back to the dealership service center with all of the latest and greatest detection devises employed and nothing could be found. At this point, the dealership owner instructed the service department to take the car apart to find the noise. After disassembling the backseat passenger's door which seemed to be the general location of the rattle, then cutting open a sealed panel, an empty soda pop bottle was exposed with a note inside which read "bet it took a long time to find this."

Management vs worker problems, like this, became a frequent occurrence in the 1970's which then became dubbed the Lordstown Syndrome, which is named after the GM factory in Northeast Ohio. In the 1970s, the factory's 7,000 workers were so bitter toward management thousands of Chevrolet Vegas rolled off the assembly line with slit upholstery and other damage. The hostility eventually led to a 22-day strike in 1972 costing G.M. $150 million, and the term "Lordstown Syndrome" became shorthand to describe damages resulting from antagonistic relationship between management and factory workers.

When employee's thoughts, opinions, and contributions are ignored, they usually react in negative ways to get attention.

119

Employee's who are not recognized for the positive contributions to the organization, will begin to get bored and turn their creative talents into other directions, such as finding ways to get recognition for negative behavior. All employees need to receive feedback, recognition, and new challenges at their job. When they don't, they will find other avenues to receive personal fulfillment – whether it is conducting personal business on company time, organizing sport pools, or nuisance sabotage. The smarter employees will be the most creative with their personal exploits costing the employer lost productivity. Cost associated with such behavior is very hard to track. It is essentially white-collar crime which is seldom gets detected.

If a human does not receive recognition for desired behavior; they will pursue recognition for undesired behavior

You were born with two eyes; two ears; and one mouth; use them in that proportion.

Chapter Six

JULIE

Through the years, I have received invitations to speak at numerous organizations throughout the US on a wide variety of business topics. When such requests are offered, my typical routine is to collect details, their meeting goals, what they want to accomplish with the presentation, location, etc. submit a contract, and place the information in a labeled file folder, enter date and location on my calendar.

Since these commitments are usually made over a year in advance, I do not get into the details of the presentation until the date gets close enough to start making travel arrangements, specific audience needs, etc. On one such occasion, I accepted an opportunity to speak at a business convention in Florida. When the date of the Florida meeting was within my infamous "it is time to start making travel arrangements" I went through my notes in the file folder and realized I had agreed to do my "How to Treat Your Employees like a Dog" presentation and agreed to have one of my dogs as a co-presenter.

This was not unusual; I have dealt with similar situations in the past, no problem. But the date of the Florida program was tightly wedged between dates where I was to be thousands of miles away. Normally when I do presentations with a dog as part of the program, I drive. This was not going to be a drive-to opportunity. It required flying to Florida. I really did not like the idea of kenneling my dogs in the lower belly, luggage compartment of the plane. Fortunately the airline was very cooperative and worked with me, so Julie could fly with me, at my feet in coach.

Julie was a 55-pound golden retriever, with a very thick white coat and though she was five years old at the time she retained a very cute puppy face.

Julie was a very confident dog who walked with a saunter of a life-long celebrity. She had come to us from a breeder known for producing obedience dogs, so Julie was easy to train and had numerous obedience titles. She was accustomed to crowded buildings, unusual noises, and the approach of strangers to pet or meet her. It was always flattering to have Julie as my partner because she always made me look good. Julie was a well-trained, confident dog, capable of laying at my feet on a three-hour flight to Florida, making me look good the entire trip.

On the day of the flight, I arrived at the airport, parked my car in the airport parking lot, took Julie, my luggage, her luggage, her carry-on bag, and my back pack and walked to the terminal. We checked the appropriate luggage with the ticket agent, who could not have been nicer, and headed for a last outdoor Julie rest stop before heading to our gate. I have spent most of my professional career, over 40 years, traveling for business, by air, millions of miles, thousands of times, in a variety of airports, but by far, this was the most pleasant experience I ever had. Everyone was so friendly.

With Julie in hand, we traversed the airport as customers smiled and opened walk ways for us to pass through. Virtually everyone we passed smiled at us. Many offered friendly greetings, including airport staff and security. It is amazing how much nicer people respond to me traveling with a dog than they had when I was alone.

Next was the process of going through TSA security, I received the usual shake down, emptying pockets, back pack; walk through the metal detector, in contrast, Julie was escorted by a TSA agent around the metal detector while a variety of TSA officers fawned over her verbally and physically. People were petting her, talking baby talk to her, while I was retrieving belts, shoes and electronic items off the conveyor belt. After re-dressing and re-packing I had to work my way through a crowd who were fussing over Julie, to be re-united. At this point, I was beginning to understand what it must feel like to be the spouse of a famous celebrity.

We arrived at our gate and checked in with the attending agent. The flight had begun loading passengers, but before sending us down the jet way, the gate agent contacted the flight crew concerning Julie's arrival. A flight attendant met us as we boarded the jet, escorted us to our seat, but before allowing us to sit, she announced to the boarded passengers, a dog would be sitting in the bulk head row and if anyone in the surrounding area was uncomfortable, she would provide other seating options.

It was just the opposite; we had an overwhelming response of passengers asking to sit next to the dog. As it turned out, there was a petite woman, in her eighties, in the seat directly next to us, who then stood up and announced she wanted to sit next to the dog and no one was going to get her seat. End of discussion.

I sat down in my aisle bulkhead seat; Julie took her place at my feet on the floor. After all of the passengers had boarded the plane I noticed one of the pilots in the cockpit looking over his shoulder down the main aisle at us. I tried not to make eye contact, and tried to position Julie so she was not visible to the pilot. It was about that time the pilot stood up from his seat, departed the cockpit, walked down the center aisle directly toward us. He stood in the aisle directly next to me, looking down at Julie and I, then in a very professional, somber, military sounding voice said "Good afternoon sir". My heart rate is racing; blood pressure is on the rise, thinking to myself, what trouble am I in now?

As I looked up to make eye contact, with a smile and responded to the pilot's greeting, he then knelt down on the floor next to me and in front of Julie. At this point, the pilot proceeded to pet Julie while talking baby talk about having his own dog and this is how his dog liked to be petted. Believe it or not it gets better. The pilot then pulls out his wallet to show Julie a picture of his dog and explains how his dog likes to chase tennis balls, once again, in baby talk, asking Julie if she likes chasing tennis balls?

Shortly after the tennis ball conversation someone in the cockpit signaled Julie's new pilot friend back to the cockpit, he continued using baby talk conversation with Julie explaining he had to go fly the plane. At the conclusion of his conversation with Julie, the pilot stood straight up, next to my seat, looking down at me and in his serious military voice and said "Thank you, sir, I have to return to the cockpit". This is the guy who is flying the plane. The day was getting more surreal by the minute.

The aircraft pulled away from the gate, taxied to the runway and became airborne without any complications. Shortly after the pilot departed for the cockpit the 80-year-old woman sitting next to me, began talking to Julie. She told Julie about her life. The woman recalled, by name, all of the dogs she had ever owned with stories about each. Then she told Julie about the dogs her daughters own, their names and ages. About midway into the flight, the woman believed Julie wanted to look out the window next to her, so she could see the clouds. I assured her, Julie did not need to see the clouds, but the woman persisted, so I gave in, lifted Julie to the window to look out at the clouds, which is when the woman told Julie stories about the clouds. Other than the few short episodes where the woman stopped for refreshments, she talked to Julie the entire flight telling her stories of her life.

During the flight, I had several passengers seated near us get up from their seats to offer their airline pretzels to Julie or ask to pet her. We landed on time and taxied to the gate. Since I was in an aisle seat I was one of the first to stand. Asking the woman if she had a bag in the overhead luggage compartment, she explained its appearance, which was easy to locate. I pulled it down and gave it to her. Then I instructed Julie to get up so we could prepare to deplane. This is when the most remarkable experience of the entire day occurred. The 80-year-old woman grabbed Julie around the neck, hugged her, gave her a kiss and said to Julie, "Thank you, this has been one of the most enjoyable days I have had in years."

As is too often the case, instead of recognizing what I had just witnessed, I was preoccupied with all of the trivial activities in life, getting off the plane, finding Julie an exercise area, picking up our checked luggage, finding the rental car desk, etc., etc. So, it wasn't until hours later, of the 80 year old woman's parting comment to Julie, I finally got it. What had Julie done to make this 80-year-old woman's day so great?

She listened.

THAT WAS IT------SHE LISTENED!!!

How often in life do we find anyone who is willing to listen to anything we have to say? Let alone listen for hours. Listening may be the greatest form of flattery you can provide to another person. Listening to someone else means we have to put aside your own ego, your own needs, just to listen to someone else. Taking the time required to sincerely listen, while someone else is speaking their thoughts, is a true compliment which does not come naturally.

VICTOR

Victor was a sales rep I inherited as sales manager. He was not a very impressive person physically. Victor was short and had a pudgy, apple-like shape body, with thinning hair. He was always well dressed and neat, but not extravagant or flashy. Victor was simple in appearance, yet confident in his manners.

Victor had immigrated to the US and had a heavy accent, which for most people was hard to understand. In addition, I am not sure if it was a speech impediment or difficulty enunciating words, making it challenging to understand most of what he said. When Victor spoke, I had to pay close attention to understand what he was saying. I tried very hard not to embarrass him by constantly asking if he would repeat what he had just said. After spending time with him, I realized Victor was very aware people had difficulty understanding him He was self-conscious of his ability to verbalize thoughts, which is why, I believe, he limited his contributions during conversations. He seldom spoke and when he did it was in very short statements. He worked very hard to speak slowly and enunciate words to help other understand.

So then, how is it Victor was the top sales person in the company? Not the top sales man for one week, or for one month, or even for one year, but for many years? As a sales manager, it is important to ride with reps to insure they are using sales material properly, making the appropriate sales calls, and make sure the field sale representatives are doing their jobs. Before meeting with Victor on this trip, as I would do before riding with any sales rep, I reviewed his past sales and performance. Having knowledge of Victor's past performance, I was very interested to learn what made him so successful. And now after meeting him for the first time, I was a bit perplexed. How did this guy sell anything? Victor certainly did not fit the stereotypical image of a top sales person.

The first time I met Victor, my plan was to spend the day working with him making sales calls with him in his territory. It was the usual start to the day, where we met at a coffee shop during which Victor described the calls he had set up for the day. I was to simply ride with him and observe the knowledge he had of his territory, customers, and products. He had appointments set, so we headed out to the first customer's office. When we arrived, Victor parked the car and pulled out a file of past calls, two years of sales were broken down by product, by week, and other documents related to this specific customer. He reviewed information as to what was discussed in past calls with this customer, what products the customer was using, and the growth potential this customer possessed.

Victor had kept a detailed history of his past experiences with this customer and his plan of action to build sales. He was very well prepared and everything he did indicated his years of experience. We walked into the first office and it was obvious by the smiles, comments, and body language the staff in this office knew Victor. The wait wasn't long and we were escorted back to the customer's office.

I introduced myself, but based on the smiles, handshakes, pats on each other's backs, etc., Victor and the customer knew each other well. So far, so good. Everything I saw to this point was typical customer, sales person behavior. But, what was the magic that made Victor a better sales person than anyone else?

Now for the moment of truth, it was time for the actual sales presentation. Most commonly, a sales call begins with the sales person initiating the conversation utilizing a general benefit statement (an opener summarizing past conversations or future opportunities) followed by the featured product introduction. But before Victor said a word, the customer was eager to begin speaking:

Customer:

Since your last sales visit, I have tried your new product.

Victor's response:

OH? (as Victor slightly tilted his head with an inquisitive look on his face)

Customer:

It is a bit different than I have been used to with similar products, but I did find it to have some interesting qualities.

Victor:

OOOOOOHHH? (as Victor leaned forward in his chair, looking directly at the customer, while slightly nodding his head up and down.)

Customer:

It seems your product has a broader variety of applications. We found....

Victor:

OHHH! (as Victor raised his eyebrow, widen his eyes, growing smile on his face, and nodded his head up and down as to agree with the customer)

Customer:

So I am not the first person to recognize these benefits? As the customer continues going into great detail as to the uses and successes his company's staff had with our product.

Victor:

OH!! (as Victor's smile grew to a grin and with an agreeing head nod becoming stronger)

Customer:

That is interesting to learn. Have others.....

Are you starting to get the picture? Victor's complete repertoire of speech during the vast majority of sales interaction with customers was one word, "Oh". But each "Oh" sounded completely different due to his voice inflection, body posture, facial gestures, and overall appearance. Victor could make "Oh" sound like a question asking for more information; or supportive statement to build confidence and rewarding desired behavior; or with a slight chuckle to break tension; or with a sigh offering empathy and sincerity. Also important to understand, throughout this sale call; Victor is taking copious written notes of the customer's comments.

As you have probably already guessed, my day with Victor continued as it started, the rest of customer visits were a repeat of the first sales call. The man had perfected the use of the word "Oh" It wasn't the word "Oh" making Victor successful, it was how he personalized each "Oh" with so many of the little things in communication, transmitting feelings and emotion. Like great actors, it is not the words they speak, but more importantly, it is how they package those words with voice, tone, and body language to convey to their audience far more than any words can describe. Each "Oh" provided more information than just one word because of the manner in which Victor presented it.

In addition to having excellent skills at asking questions and providing a forum for customers to share information, Victor created a safe environment for the customer to speak honestly. Victor's non-threatening appearance and sincerely warm demeanor created an environment where customers wanted to share information. Such information increases in value when recorded for future sales calls, which Victor did throughout the meeting, and generated useful product information to be shared with other company personnel. This, too, was a strength Victor possessed.

After each sales call, he returned to the car to record pertinent customer comments which he had written during the sales call. Keeping accurate records of each sales call in a well-organized customer filling system was another important building block to Victors continued success. Customers loved Victor and his sales call visits because he listened to them. If you remember at the beginning of the first sales call, the customer was anxious to start the conversation, telling of their success with Victor's product before Victor even had a chance to initiate a general benefit statement. This is because during past visits, the customer had been rewarded by Victor's sincere interest to listen.

We all enjoy hearing ourselves speak and believe everyone else should want to hear what we have to say. Victor provided each of his customers the respect of sincere listening. By his listening, Victor had trained his customers to provide a great deal of information about their use of his products and opportunities for more sales. The smiles and head nods were all positive reinforcement the customer enjoyed receiving and wanted to experience more often.

Victor had trained his customers with positive reinforcement, similar to a dog trainer giving food to a dog after performing a desired behavior. Also important, while the customer was telling Victor the uses they have for his products, he is able to learn more about the customer's needs. He also learned alternative uses of his product which might be helpful to other customers. Having earned the respect of his customers by being a superb listener, when Victor did speak customers patiently listened with serious interest while Victor slowly enunciating difficult to understand words while employing visual aides to support the claims and information he was introducing.

Victor knew the sales support materials inside and out. When he needed to answer a customer's question, he went to the best materials to answer specific questions and with pen in hand pointed out the answers. Victor compensated for his verbal issues by having explicit command of the visual aids, clinical studies, and other sales materials at his disposal. His materials were strategically arranged by Victor in his brief case. He could pull out what he needed while never taking his eyes off of the customer. When the opportunity was just right, he pointed to the specific answer with the point of his pen or with that same pen he circled the area on which he wanted the customer to focus attention.

A picture is worth 1000 words.

This way, Victor was able to answer questions quickly and accurately, without having to speak very often. Because Victor created an environment where customers felt important and he showed how much he cared about them by sincerely listening, his customers trusted him and wanted him to be successful. Everything about Victor's behavior was professional.

On one of the sales calls, Victor used as his general benefits statement "How would you use this?" when he handed the customer a sample of a new product we were introducing. Then Victor pulled out his paper and pen to take notes. The customer studied the new product for a while until he had formulated an opinion. Victor never rushed the customer for an answer, nor did he act impatient. He gave the customer time so when the customer began to explain in detail where it would fit into his company's needs, Victor's behavior, of taking notes, was supportive and with sincere interest.

Victor directed and controlled the conversation utilizing his skills with open ended questions and non-verbal gestures, Victor maneuvered the customer into a position where he simply closed the sale with a close-ended question "How many will you need to start this process?" (Such a question may be referred to as an assumptive close.)

Needless to say, my first day riding with Victor was truly a learning experience, not just in sales skills, but also and more importantly in people skills.

Neurolinguistics

How the typical human Interprets spoken communication is:

7% Words

38% Tone and voice inflection

55% Body language

Some studies believe body language can represent as much as 75% of communication. Like humans, dog communication is heavily dependent on interpreting body language and behavior, but instead of using words in communication, dogs depend more on smell and other sounds, such as tone and inflection. It is easy to lie using just words. But, body language, smells, tone and inflection are far more difficult to disguise one's true feelings.

After a conversation with another person have you ever said, "They said all of the right things, but I just did not believe them?" It is probably because the person's body language did not match their spoken words. Most people have a difficult time hiding their true emotions while they are lying. Your words need to match your emotions and feelings to be believed.

Victor also used his neurolinguistics skills to maximize his question asking. When he leaned forward toward the customer he was non-verbally saying I am interested -- keep talking. The same is true when he would smile, another non-verbal signal encouraging the customer to elaborate on the current subject matter. Even simple gestures such as raised eyebrows and slightly enlarged eyes will signal to the speaker the listener is interested and wants to hear more. The reverse is also true. If the listener wants to signal to the speaker they are uninterested, then they would simply lean away from the speaker, looking away, frowning or lowing the eyebrows and shrinking the size of the exposed eyeball. These are all gestures that non-verbally say we disagree of do not have interest.

Questions

Victor used his body language to control the conversation as much as any spoken words. To be a good listener first requires the ability to get others talking. But even more important is to get people talking about subjects of importance to the listener, which requires the skill of asking effective questions.

It takes preparation and training to become good at the skill of asking questions. Knowing how to phrase a question requires planning, evaluating and testing. Structuring an effective question is a skill very few people possess. Using the most effective words to achieve the desired result of a question is critical to asking a question. A common problem people have is the skill of knowing when to ask an open-ended question versus asking a close-ended question. Asking challenging questions stimulates thought and produces informative answers. It takes thought provoking open-ended questions to get through superficial conversation or objections and uncover a person's real need, opportunity or problem.

Open-ended Questions

Asking questions is like peeling and onion. Initial questions are usually most effective if they are phrased as open ended. Open-ended questions are those which cannot be answered with one word, they require a longer description. Open-ended questions force respondents to elaborate on thoughts and feelings. These are questions which usually include the words such as what, how, tell me about, explain, etc., even as simple a word as "Oh" can be an effective open-ended question. If each question is successful, it will peel off another layer of the onion. It will get the questioner another step closer to the heart of the onion, which is the respondent's true issue, problem or opportunity. Notice the number of open-ended questions which were asked by Victor, and how much information the customer was willing to share.

Close-ended Questions

Close-ended questions are those which can be answered with a one-word answer, such as yes, no, six, never, etc. Close-ended questions are most effective when used to confirm already gathered information or when you are close to the heart or core of the onion (issue, problem, or opportunity). Close-ended questions are very useful when confirming a presumed need, problem, or opportunity has been uncovered. Close-ended questions are used by the questioner as a test to confirm an identified need, opportunity, or problem.

Great leaders, successful sales people, effective police investigators, or trial lawyers usually possess the skill of asking poignant questions requiring additional deeper thought. An effective question should stimulate thought and cause people to think deeply to formulate an answer. The second component to asking an effective question is the ability to be a great listener.

Listening

Research has found the most successful sales people spend 75% or more of their time in front of customers listening and less than 25% talking. In contrast, people who have short careers in sales spend 90% or more of their time in front of the customer talking and less than 10% allowing the customer to speak. This only makes sense because we cannot learn while talking. Learning requires listening.

Those who talk the most usually have the least to say.

Who is the most interesting person you have ever met?
You!
We all love to talk about ourselves.

At the start of the work day in just about every office, someone can be heard saying: "Let me tell you what happened to me on the way to work this morning" which is soon followed by: "That's nothing, from a co-worker; wait till you hear what happened to me." We love to talk about ourselves, because we are the most interesting person we know. We spend more time talking about ourselves than talking about anything else. It is for these reasons sincerely listening naively is difficult.

To listen, we have to put someone else's needs ahead of ourselves. Setting our ego aside and turning our interest to another person is not easy. Listening is not passive activity; it's actually a lot of work.

There are three levels of listening

- Not hearing
- Hearing but not listening
- Active listening

Active listening causes the heart rate to increase, respiration to increase, and blood pressure to rise. Active listening requires focusing our full attention on what someone else is saying. Active listening is so difficult most people can only do it for mere minutes at a time without lapsing into intermediate daydreams, or search for past experience or prepare a response. The average brain is capable of processing approximately 500 words per minute, yet the average person speaks at a rate of about 200 words per minute – leaving a lot of spare brain time (about 300 words per minute) to think about other things. It takes discipline to listen, because our spare brain time wants to think about other things. With the extra space, our brains wants to start thinking about what we are going to do this evening, or a phone call we need to return, or the coffee stain on the shirt of the person who is talking.

Even more important is learning to listen naively. Listening naively requires a commitment to listen without trying to formulate a response until the speaker has completed their thought. We all have prejudices and frames of reference from previous life experiences. Unfortunately, those experiences come into play with every communication experience in life. Becoming a naïve listener requires the discipline of not jumping to conclusions or finishing other's sentences, which is difficult with 300 words per minute of unused brain space. It is very easy to hear a word or phrase, which then sends our brain spinning off thinking about something other than what the speaker is intending, which is when we sabotage the intent of the message.

The most important component of communications is listening.

Great listeners need to possess the ability to listen with an open mind if they hope to learn anything. Listening to another person's full thought without jumping to conclusions is critical to effective communication. How often have you been in a conversation where the person you are speaking with finishes your sentences? This is not listening. To listen naively requires control of emotions. Reacting to preconceived emotions can cause us to begin formulating a response, rather than listening to full thoughts. When listening to another person, our natural human reaction is to respond quickly.

A magnificently presented question in which no one listens for an answer was just a waste of time and energy. Listening is an even more important skill than the ability to ask a well-structured, properly positioned question. Another trait possessed by great listeners is the ability to be patient. After asking a useful question, too often the askers get impatient while the potential responder formulates an answer. The questioner winds up answering their own question.

Answering your own question is insulting to the other person in the conversation. Not providing another person the time to formulate an answer and respond does not provide an opportunity to learn anything. After asking a challenging question a second of silences seems like five minutes and a minute of silence seems like an hour. The ability to wait patiently, quietly and confidently with sincere interest while another person contemplates their answer takes discipline and practice. While you sit quietly waiting for a response to your question, your brain now has 500 words per minute of unused brain space which is impatiently waiting to be used.

Tools to improving listening include

Asking questions

Taking notes

Reporting learned information back to others

How to handle an angry customer

Listening is the foundation for defusing an angry customer. When a customer is angry their body is usually secreting a large amount of adrenaline. Adrenaline causes the body to revert to primal instincts: fight, flight, or freeze. This means the brain stops cognitive reasoning.

This is an explanation for road rage – in a split second, the secretory blast of adrenaline into the blood stream causes people to react without contemplating the outcome of their actions. People for whom a blast of adrenaline produces fight when angered or scared are not rational when they register a product or service complaint. They are raging in irrational anger. This is where listening becomes the foundation for converting a complaint into a productive customer interaction. When faced with an angry customer, the first step is to let the customer speak freely. Do not try to employ the art of debate with an adrenaline-enraged customer. When a person is in an adrenal-induced rage, they are in search of a good fight. Those who try to correct an angry customer with facts are simply adding more adrenaline to the customer's blood stream.

Do not try to talk rationally with an angry customer until they have fully vented all of their venom. After the customer has fully burnt off of their anger and their adrenaline is under control, it is time to accept responsibility and apologize for the customer's problem. Do not blame anyone else. Diverting the blame for the problem to someone else only makes you look weak and incompetent. Simply and confidently apologize. It is human instinct to forgive others.

139

A sincere apology usually turns an angry customer into a caring human being. Be sure the customer has calmed down to a state of sanity before you proceed. If you try to apologize while the customer is in an adrenaline rage, their anger will further heighten. After the customer has calmed down, and they have accepted your apology it is time to move into step three. Once the customer is conversing in a sane manner, it is time to create an action plan.

Ask the customer how they would like the problem corrected. When given this option, most customers will respond with a workable solution. Listen naively to the customer's suggestions to resolve their problem, then using the information and working within company policy to formulate a plan of action. Once the plan is agreed upon, everyone knows what to expect and what to do.

Most people who complain are doing so because they feel disrespected and unrecognized. Providing recognition and respect through listening is the most effective method of disarming such anger.

Steps to handling an angry customer

1. Listen
2. Accept responsibility and apologize
3. Create a plan of action

Listening is the most important, critical step to defusing the problem.

Psychotherapy

The science of psychotherapy was built on the premise of asking a patient questions and allowing the patient to talk freely so they can express not just their problems, but also the cause of their problems. With the appropriate, directive questions followed by time to formulate answers, the patient will find answers to their problems. If I tell you how to solve your problems, you do not have to believe me. In fact, if someone else tells you your problems and how to correct your problems you will probably resent such opinions and do the opposite.

The only person who can solve your problems is you.

But, if **you** identify your own problems and then create solutions to them, then you believe it and will be much more committed to invest your time and energy putting your solution into effect.

Using Listening to Control Behavior

Defuse problems

Continue desired behavior

Extinguish undesired behavior

Like Julie and Victor, good listeners are:

Good listeners are well liked.

Good listeners tend to be successful.

Good listeners usually control meeting and conversation because they ask challenging questions, thus directing conversation.

Good listeners make the best leaders because they are always learning.

Good listeners make better decisions because they are successful in collecting information.

Good listeners are respected.

Good listeners are appreciated.

It is better to be thought the fool; than to speak and prove it.

The most common reason people quit a job: incompetent direct supervisor.

Chapter Seven

Marty

A call came into Golden Retriever Rescue inquiring how to handle a dog that was being turned in by its owner. It was from the dog's original owners who had found their dog to be dangerous. So arrangements were made for the owners to deliver their dog to our house.

The dog was a 75-pounds, 24 inches at the withers (which is term used to describe a dogs height measuring from ground to the top of the dogs shoulders), strawberry blond, 10 months old, goofy, Golden Retriever. Like most Golden Retrievers, just a big happy, high energy, bounding dog. The owners were very frustrated with the destructive behavior of their dog and they could no longer tolerate having him in their house. They described the dog as out of control and his behavior to be unpredictable. Fearing he might bite and simply stated they did not trust him.

At the same time, the owners were describing their dog's behavior, I was watching their children climb out of the back windows of the car and walking on the roof of their car, not listening to their parent's shouting commands to behave.

Between shouting at his children to behave, the husband/father stated "we paid $800 for this dog eight months ago, but we cannot tolerate his behavior," as if the cost of the dog is an indicator of the animal's social skills. They were correct the dog did not have any obedience training, but nor did their children. The exchange took place on our driveway, and we assured the family their dog would have a good life and waited until they drove out of sight before we introduced him to the members of his new pack.

Whenever we bring in a new dog into our pack that has had a history of behavior problems, we want to start by changing its name. By re-training a name we are trying to create a new mind set for a new environment. So we named him Marty. Why Marty? Because he looked and acted like a Marty.

The next step was for Marty to meet his new pack – our four resident dogs. This was done one at a time, outside, on the driveway, with everyone on leash to insure control of the initial meet and greets. The introductions were typical Golden Retriever initial encounters, one by one the four spayed females sniffing and licking the new male roommate. After all of the dogs had a chance to introduce themselves without any conflict, we allowed them to spend some time together as a group on the driveway and evaluate their pack hierarchy. Dogs, like people, will after a short interaction, determine what place in the pack each fits.

We very quickly learned Marty was scared or distrustful of me (the human male in the pack). So, Marty was on constant alert to keep his distance from me. He would try to stay 12-15 feet away from me. After we went into our house, Marty continued to keep his distance from me, in some cases moving to an adjoining room in the house and observing me through doorways. As I moved from one location in the house to another, so did Marty keeping his distance and ensuring he knew where I was at all times.

The second behavior Marty exhibited was his interest to steal our shoes or socks then dance in front of us to show off his prized items. Marty did not hide the fact he had an item with a human scent in his mouth, and he wanted to be sure we knew what he was doing.

The third behavior Marty displayed was a fear of being petted especially when the approach came from above his head. When a human would try to pet Marty by touching him on the top of the head, he would very quickly dodge, bob, and retreat. Any movement by a human to move toward his head or neck area resulted in a semi-fearful, semi-playful escape.

The original owners provided us with a file of information regarding the eight months they had Marty, including veterinarian notes. Some of these documents included how the original owners were told to gain control over Marty they needed to **force** him on his back with his belly up. This was supposed to show Marty who was the boss, and he needed to be submissive to his human family member. Forcing Marty, or any animal on his back, does just the opposite. It caused him to react fearfully and violently to get out of such a vulnerable situation. Forcing any animal on its back is very threatening and scary. The natural response to being forced into a vulnerable position is retaliation to regain a safer positon such as standing. The natural response to any threat, whether we are talking human or dog is Fight, Flight, or Freeze.

Those options applied especially when forced into an upside-down-feet-in-the-air position. Marty's retaliatory reaction, attempting to return to his standing feet on the ground, when they would force him on his back, was interpreted by his first family as being aggressive. In Marty's veterinarian records, it was also recommended to euthanize him for being aggressive.

Based on the short observation of Marty's first family, the four members all treated Marty differently. There was no consistency of rules or expected behavior. They also lacked leadership. So Marty never received any consistent training, but instead, a wide variety of directives from everyone in the family. Marty would get petted for doing something one day, and then reprimanded the next day for the same behavior based on the person who was closest to him. The parents kept changing their treatment of Marty based on the suggestions of their veterinarian, friends, neighbors, etc.

At first, as a puppy, they found Marty's behavior to be cute and entertaining, then as time passed they began chasing him with anger, when caught, forcing Marty into a submissive position with belly up. Marty did not know how to react, or who to trust.

It is very common for people to adopt a puppy at roughly 8 weeks of age. At such an early age they are so cute, fuzzy, warm, mouthy puppies with baby teeth. Puppies, even though they bite and chew, can't do much damage. The new adopters of this cute puppy found all of these behaviors as adorable and entertaining. But as time progressed, the puppy grows larger, and puppy teeth are replaced by adult teeth, which now can do a lot more damage. Like children who experience teething, comfort comes from chewing, so they want to mouth and chew.

While children who experience the teething process are given a variety of items to chew to comfort their discomfort, unfortunately, most dog owners do not pick up on the teething dog's needs. So when dog chew toys are not readily available, and the teething puppy is not taught what chew options are acceptable, dogs search for things like wood cabinets, furniture, shoes, etc. to satisfy their teething need. This type of destructive behavior then leads the owner to anger over the damage caused by the growing puppy's teething chew drive. As the dog grows larger, so, too, does the destruction they can inflict in both in size and cost.

Such was the case with Marty in his first family. Marty would find a great chew toy such as a really nice leather shoe, or wonderful soft smelly sock. The next thing to happen in Marty's life would be a human starts yelling and chasing him, which to Marty was now a game. The game of chase consisted of picking up a human-smelling item, show it to the humans, then they begin chasing and yelling. What great fun for a 6-month old puppy; life does not get much better! The more chasing, the more yelling, the angrier the humans became and the more intensified the game became. The humans did not understand their reaction was reinforcing Marty's behavior. The attention of chasing Marty when he had a human item simply encouraged him to continue such behavior.

Marty was smart enough to know how to use his speed and quickness compared to his human pursuers. So he would allow those chasing him to get close enough for them to lunge with their hand for his collar, then at the last second, he would react with a dodge, bob, or weave movement to elude his pursuers. This must have been his greatest play game – steal a valuable item which then stimulates humans to chase. Show the humans you have their treasured possession, then run, let the humans chase, allow them to get close enough they can grab for your collar and then, at the last second, with the elusiveness of an NFL all-pro running back escape capture. Repeat.

In most dog homes, the most athletic pursuer of stolen items is Dad. Dad is typically the biggest, strongest member of the family and provides the best challenge in the game of chase the dog. In most cases of families owning a pet, Dad is also the human with severest temper and takes on the responsibility for inflicting punishment for misbehavior. In Marty's case, Dad was probably the human who provided the most aggressive chase and hand lunging in an effort to snag the misbehaving dog. When Marty did get caught with the stolen item, Dad was probably the family member responsible for instituting the punishment. Marty's distrust of me was probably due to the behavior of his first family's adult male behavior toward him.

Once Marty was in our house, his new foster home, chasing and yelling at dogs was not a game we humans played. It did not take Marty long to employ his play game of steal an item which smelled like a human, show it to the human, and start the game of chase. I am sure he was thinking, I wonder how good these humans are at the game of chase. Since our four dogs have never received any reward to participate in such a game, they were not interested to initiate similar types of behavior, or even aid and abet in the activity. Marty must have been amazed to find clothes closets with shoes on the floor, easy pickings for an experienced 10-month-old thief.

Within hours of being in our house, Marty grabbed one of Bonnie's shoes, and then strutted off to the family room where we could be found. By this time he was all excited and ready for the fun to begin. On his first pass by us he did not receive any reaction. At this point Marty had to be thinking these stupid humans are going to require a lot of chase training. On his next pass, he came closer to us to ensure we saw what was in his mouth. Once again, the humans did not react as he expected. Instead, Bonnie walked over to a dog biscuit jar in the family room, at which time all four of our dogs immediately responded with interest – rushing to sit-in-front position.

She then called Marty, who showed no interest. Why should he? He was in charge with the chase bait, right? Bonnie then asked the four dogs to sit, they did, and she gave them each a dog biscuit. Meanwhile, Marty stood on the other side of the room looking very confused. Then Bonnie gave the four female dogs a command to down, all four promptly laid down, followed by each receiving verbal praise and a second dog biscuit, This further confused Marty. He finally dropped the shoe and walked away totally disappointed at the human response to his chase play effort. This was a good learning experience for us; we now found one of Marty's undesirable learned behaviors. After the first shoe thievery incident ,we placed any shoes of value out of Marty's reach, leaving low value shoes with our scent in places he had access to so we could continue the training. Marty did not disappoint, he made his second shoe abduction, expecting to receive the same kind of reaction he had become so programed to expect from his first home. But once again these new humans did not react the same way.

Instead, Bonnie, as she did the first time this happened, called the other four dogs to front and gave those treats. I am sure Marty was thinking, "What is wrong with these humans?" "Why don't they understand how to play the chase game?" He probably was also confused the female dogs, in our pack, were not any better. They didn't steal shoes, they didn't even get excited when Marty would offer the shoes as chase toys to them.

Over the course of the next several days the same pattern continued, Marty would steal a shoe, expect a chase, the other dogs would be called to front and receive dog biscuits. Marty would look on from across the room, shoe in mouth, totally confused. The rules had changed and he was trying to figure out what went wrong. About the 15th shoe theft episode, Marty decided while the female dogs were receiving their second treats he might want to get on the food. He dropped the shoe and came to Bonnie to see if he, too, could receive a dog biscuit. He did receive a treat, and some learning (re-programing) just took place.

In about five days, the shoe stealing stopped all together.

Due to the distrust Marty initially displayed toward me, (the male human in the house), it was important to start training with Bonnie providing the dog biscuit rewards. Because he so strongly indicated distrust toward me, we did not want to further threaten him. He perceived Bonnie as less of a threat, so she handled virtually all interaction with Marty.

Change what behavior is rewarded; change behavior

The next step was to build trust between Marty and me, which would take some time. I had to let him initiate a relationship. The first step was to prepare and feed Marty all of his meals, which was simply putting food in his dish and placing the food dish in his crate. He was not yet ready to eat from my hand this kind of trust would take time to build. It took more than a week before Marty would move to the same room I was in. I continued not to make any quick movements toward him, and over time he began to believe I could be trusted. I tried to let him make all of the advances to establish a relationship.

The distance between he and I continued to get closer until one day he approached me while I was working at my desk in my office with my back toward the room entry. Marty came in and sat next to the chair in which I was sitting. I did not attempt to pet him or make contact. But after he offered such behavior, I began feeding him his meals by hand, which further built the trust between us. Even at this point, I still did not approach him; I always let him approach me.

Although we had overcome the steal to chase behavior and the fear of adult male human behavior, Marty continued to back away from any attempt to pet the top of his head or reach over his head or collar. We continued to only pet Marty after he approached us, and only on the chest and side. Overcoming the fear of being grabbed by the collar to be reprimanded took much longer, which again only occurs after establishing confidence nothing bad is going to happen.

After living with us for several months, Marty began to trust us to pet him on the top of his head and even reach for his collar. Marty's trust and confidence in his new pack got stronger and he would voluntarily roll on his back to have us rub his chest and belly. This is very different than the forced roll over of placing an animal in a very vulnerable position. When an animal rolls on their back of their own free will, they are acknowledging they not only trust those around them but are also acknowledging themselves to be subordinate.

It was at this point Marty became eligible to be adopted.

Respect is earned through consistency

Marty went on to his new home and had a great life. He became a loved member of their family. There were never any reports of destructive or aggressive behavior. Marty, like all of us, wanted and needed consistent leadership in his life.

Charlie

Having been a field sales person or sales manager for 42 years, I have visited a lot of companies. What I have learned is organizations tend to take on the personality of its leadership. When I see staff acting non-expressive, non-reactive, gray-faced, and emotionless, I refer to this type of employee as "drones", it's the result of an unpredictable leader. In most cases, these employees do not make eye contact. They seldom initiate conversation. Walking through the various departments of such companies is depressing and perpetuates a feeling of dread. By simply observing the behavior of staff, it becomes easy to predict the behavior of the leader. That was Charlie, who was the owner of a manufacturing company.

Charlie was inconsistent. Sometimes he showed up for work early, sometimes late. Sometimes he walked into the office with a smile on his face, happy, gleeful, and pleasant to spend time with; other days he would enter the office quiet with a scowl, not responding to any greetings. One day Charlie is telling stories to anyone who will listen, the next day he is quiet and isolates himself in his office. There were days employees would receive compliments for their work from Charlie; other days they would be greeted with a severe reprimand for the exact same work.

It wasn't the employee's performance was any different from one day to the next; it was dependent on the mood Charlie was in at that exact moment. His behavior was so unpredictable to those who had worked for Charlie for any length of time; they simply gave up trying and just simply monotonously went through their daily routines as drones. If they received a compliment from Charlie when he was in a good mood it did not create any additional motivation. The same was true if the opposite occurred, if Charlie laid into an employee with a severe reprimand, it had no effect on future performance. The employee simply repeated the same monotonous behavior.

This constant change in behavior caused his staff to become distrustful and non-responsive. His staff became callus to anything happening around them. All they do is punch a clock, putting time into work to collect a paycheck. Every day, every task, with dull and boring rituals regardless of any feedback received. His staff was going through the motions of looking like they are doing something, but only the minimum was getting accomplished.

In the informal organization, Charlie was the cause for many jokes. Charlie signed the pay checks so employees were respectful to his face, but did the minimum to accomplish their jobs. The organization had no sense of team or unity. Over the course of time, new employees came into the organization and after a short time those who possessed self-confidence, ideas, and the desire to grow, would leave Charlie's Company to find another job. On a few occasions, I have met former employees of Charlie's, who found jobs in more progressive organizations with stable leadership. When reuniting with ex-Charlie employee's years later they were smiling, and enthusiastic about the success they were now enjoying.

In contrast, those employees who were lacking in confidence, with low self-esteem, tended to remain at Charlie's organization. Charlie's company was built on staffs that do not complement each other, nor do they look for opportunities to help each other. In fact, in most cases the remaining staff members were cynical, distrustful, and never seem to be happy.

I always find it sad visiting such organizations.

Dysfunctional organizations with inconsistent leadership lose their most productive employees fastest and the least productive are most likely to remain long-term.

Consistent Behavior

Consistent leadership behavior is critical to successfully gaining the trust of followers. Consistent behavior does not mean always being happy, or always complimenting people. Consistent behavior means acting in a predictable manner. There are very successful leaders who are grumpy all of the time, or are quiet or serious all the time; but they are consistent with their attitude toward staff. And, most importantly, they treat all their staff the same, all of the time. A leader's implementation of company policies needs to always be consistent toward all employees.

Consistency transforms average to excellent.

Successful leaders make decisions on behalf of their staff. They help their staff to be successful and provide them opportunities to succeed. Consistency means exactly that – recognition is given using the same understood established standards for all.

Reprimands take place when needed in the same manner using understood standards for all. Staff should never be surprised by a leader's behavior or policies. Organizations displaying consistent growth and success have consistency in their leadership.

Consistency in dog training begins with simple things such as vocabulary. For example, the word sit always means sit; or the word off always means off; or the word down always means down. So when I say lay, I should not expect the dog to lie down. But when I say down, I expect the dog to lie down. As a member of my pack, the dog deserves consistency.

Consistent Leadership = Confident followers.

When we place a foster dog in a new home, we provide the new owners with a list of words we trained and what behavior we expect from those words, so the new owners learn how to behave. Training the dog is about training the person who trains the dog.

An average dog has the intelligence to understand about 400 words; a smart dog understands about 600 words. Studies have demonstrated there are dogs able to understand as many as 1,200 words. Training a dog or leading an organization requires the leader to behave in large part, as a teacher establishing expected behavior.

In the Heidi chapter, I told the story of my first dog training class with the nuns who insisted upon learning consistent heeling footwork before allowing me to bring Heidi to class. The nuns knew consistent footwork on my part would improve the outcome of successfully training Heidi to heel. Because I had consistent footwork, Heidi always knew what to expect when my feet moved in a particular pattern. She knew in advance, by my foot work, when I was stopping, meaning it was time for her to sit in heel position. This same telegraphing of information took place prior to left turns, right turns, or about turns because the steps were always consistent. It sounds like simple behavior but it is the simple things which separating successful teams from the not so successful teams.

Employees prefer to have a leader who is consistent; than one who is right.

Consistent behavior needs to exist in any organization's leadership before pack members will follow. Little things, like what time does the leader show up for work. Is it the same every day? Is the leader the first person to arrive every day? How the leader dresses is a statement employee's observe, as well. Even the leader's office appearance is closely scrutinized by pack members.

Your current behavior toward others controls their future behavior toward you.

If dogs, children or employees do not have a leader they feel is worth following, they will take it upon themselves to become the leader – as was the case with Marty in his first family. If the formal leaders are inconsistent then dogs, children and employees will seek out an informal leader to follow. If a formal leader does not emerge pack members begin working independently, drastically reducing the packs survival. Marty's first owners were reactive and lacked consistent leadership skills, so Marty could control their behavior when he would taunt them with his playful behavior.

Remember the importance of consistent behavior.

Everyone wants loyalty, consistency and someone who won't quit; but everyone forgets that to get that person you need to be that person. Over my career I have found the organizations with consistent growth and success were also those organizations that had consistent leadership and culture.

Attracting prospective employees gets easier when organizations have consistent culture because the potential employee understands what the organization stands for. People whose values do not align with the culture of consistent organizations are less likely to pursue positions with such organizations.

Learned Helplessness

A laboratory study placed white rats in metal cages; the cages were divided in half with a short wall such that the rat could easily jump over the wall from one side to the other. The floor of the cage was made of electrical-conducting material. On a random basis, an electric shock was administered to one side of the cage. In a short period of time, the rats learned to move to the opposite side of the cage to avoid the shock. If the shock was switched to the opposite side of the cage, again the rats quickly learned how to escape the discomfort. This is called learned behavior. The rats learning sped up as the study continued switching shocks from one side to the other.

But when the shocks were administered on a random basis as to the frequency and side of the cage, it caused the rats to become confused because they could not escape the shocks. As with earlier trials the rat tries to learn a means of escaping the shock. But after repeated attempts to understand how to escape the shock, without success, sooner or later the rat simply gives up. The inconsistency of the shocks and the rat's inability to escape the pain ultimately leads to learned helplessness. In other words, the rats no longer try to escape the shock. Regardless how often the shocks are administered to the rats, they simply curl up and endure the pain.

Because of the inconsistency, the rats stop trying to find alternatives, they just give up. Learned helplessness is the scientific term for the drones I see working in Charlie's company.

Learned Behavior or Programing

Learned behavior early in life is the most deeply engrained activities, and is hardest behavior to change. The events we experience at a young age program us for life. For example, a baby learns very quickly when they cry; someone comes to the crib delivering attention. Maybe change the baby's diaper. Maybe pick them up and hold them. Maybe the responding adult would talk to the child while entertaining them with toys. But the activity after crying was a whole lot better than the quiet solitude occurring before the crying incident.

Later in life, the same baby is now a child in elementary school who finds disruptive behavior in class draws the teacher's attention. Being the center of the teacher's attention is a really good feeling. Before the disruptive behavior, the child was working quietly alone. After creating a disruption, the child became the center of attention, not just for the teacher but also for the entire class. This attention feels good which the child wants to have repeated. At age six, the child's learned behavior, being loud and/or disruptive results in desired attention. This is called learned behavior and it is how we become programed for future conduct.

In school, if the child became really disruptive, he received even more special attention, such as a trip to the principal's office. This behavior has now been repeated multiple times in a variety of ways with similar results, the child is the recipient of special attention from parents, teachers, and even the school principal. It does not take long, repeating this behavior results in rewards, which ·reinforcing learned behavior. The more frequent this behavior is repeated and rewarded; the deeper this learned behavior then becomes an engrained habit. Learned behavior has other names such as habit, rut, routine, and cognitive mapping. Whatever you want to call it, once it becomes entrenched in a brain, it is very hard to change.

In the case of Marty he learned stealing socks or shoes was rewarded with a game of chase. Prior to stealing an item, no one was paying attention to Marty. But after he had a mouth full of shoe, he became the center of attention for the entire family.

I am not advocating parents should ignore a crying baby with a wet diaper. What I am trying to promote is rewarding the baby who is lying in a crib entertaining itself with some unprovoked praise. Reward desired behavior with attention and praise. The same for finding students in the class room who are performing desired behaviors and recognizing them for that behavior. In the work environment, too seldom praise is given to productive employees because management will say that is what they are paid to do, their job, and their pay is reward enough. I have been told by people in management positions if you tell an employee they are doing a good job, the employee will then expect a raise, so never tell them anything good.

Leaders find people performing desired behavior and reward it.

It is important to understand what behavior is being consistently recognized. How we repeatedly react to another's behavior is either reinforcing (chasing a dog) that behavior to continue or extinguishing (ignoring the dog) that behavior from happening again.

Consistency is a powerful tool. How people react to another person's behavior will influence future behavior. It is important to realize each of us has the power to control other's (dog or human) behavior by the way we behave toward them. This explains why some people consistently receive the respect of others; while at the same time, another person receives the respect of no one. Each of us controls the way in which we are treated, simply by the way we treat others.

If you want consistent behavior from others, you must first display consistent behavior.

Rewards

Learning requires rewards. If participants do not receive rewards (feedback) for performing a particular behavior, they will not be motivated to conduct themselves as expected. While participating in training, when earned, they need to receive rewards. Such rewards could be as simple as feedback on performance. The purpose for keeping score of games, provide grades in school, or job evaluations is to provide feedback, which in itself is a reward. Other rewards include simple verbal comments, or non-verbal gestures. Simple as it may sound, motivation can come in the form of a comment such as "nice job", "you are doing great", "I like the way you do...", or even "thank you". These are all forms of feedback to keep participants motivated and interested. Rewards can also be more complex including pay raises, bonuses, gifts, prizes, or incentives.

Participation and motivation are much stronger when rewards are included in the training.

As a parent, teacher, manager, boss, spouse, or leader, your response to others is influencing future behavior. Be aware of what you reinforce and what you extinguish by your behavior.

To increase the frequency of behavior, you must sincerely and consistently reward the desired behavior immediately after it happens; every time. Once a behavior becomes learned and consistently repeated the reinforcement can become more infrequent. If the person providing the rewards is consistent and sincere, In a short time the behavior will increase in frequency.

To extinguish behavior, the opposite must occur. Ignore undesirable behavior or correct unwanted behavior with a reprimand. Reprimands are only effective if they occur less than once for every seven positive reinforcements. Successful shaping of behavior requires the trainer to understand the goal, have a plan, and most importantly, be consistent.

Branding

Branding is the concept of imprinting a consistent perception to a product. Branding is the expectation consumers have of a company services or products, based on consistent programing. Programing consumers of a brand requires a constant and consistent message to imprint the planned message. What consumers repeatedly experience is what they are conditioned to expect in the future. Many of the same principles used in learned behavior are also components of branding. Like companies, products, or services, we are all constantly branding ourselves based on our behavior toward others.

Charlie had branded himself as someone who was inconsistent, creating caution among those who worked for him. How you behave is constantly under the scrutiny of others. You are constantly branding yourself by your behavior.

Consistency requires accountability

Consistent leadership creates organizations displaying a culture of trust.

Consistent leadership creates organizations whose members support their leadership.

Consistent leadership creates organizations putting long term goals in front of immediate results.

Consistent leadership creates organizations with predictability expectations.

Consistent leadership creates organizations whose policies and procedures are visible to all, at all times.

Consistent leadership creates organizations attracting quality prospective workers.

Consistent leadership creates organizations in which prospects understand the expectations before they apply.

Consistent leadership creates organizations whose environment is attractive to creative thinking.

Consistent leadership creates organizations that have a recognizable and trusted cultural brand.

Culture eats strategy for breakfast.

Peter Drucker

A Goal Without a Plan; is Merely a Dream

Chapter Eight

Morgan

Morgan came to us as a foster. She had been picked up by the Humane Society as a stray running the streets. She was skinny, almost bony with very little coat, and the little coat she did have was very short and brittle hair. Due to her malnourished, skinny frame and her lack of coat, even on her tail, she looked more like a greyhound than Golden Retriever.

Morgan was the classic example of fight, flight or freeze. It became obvious very quickly, Morgan was scared of everything, and when she became scared, she ran. Which I believe is how she became a stray. She was frightened by something, started running and when she stopped she was lost. This was how she lived her life when the next frightening experience occurred, she ran again. Morgan did not run with purpose, she just ran to escape whatever scary thing may have happened.

When she came into our pack as a foster, it did not take long for the other dogs to realize Morgan was at the bottom of the pack, the Omega. And, Morgan totally understood her position in the pack. Watching her behavior with the other dogs suggested she had been in

163

other packs and knew she was at the bottom. In the years Morgan lived with us, and as many times the members of the pack changed, her position remained the same - at the bottom, as the Omega.

Whenever a new dog entered our pack, evaluation and training was needed. We conducted temperament tests to determine fear biting, aggression, fear of objects, noises, etc. We learned Morgan was not a biter, but she was scared of many things, so placing her in a new home was not going to be easy.

Training, on the other hand, showed a lot of promise. Morgan was smart, and she wanted to please. As long as the trainer was patient and positive, Morgan would work hard repeating exercises over and over without losing her desire for approval. She was very responsive to learning new things – as long as the environment stayed positive and unthreatening. Any rapid changes or thing she sensed as negative caused her brain to stop cognitive thinking, followed by the autonomic nervous system response of flight. My slightest change in emotion was interpreted by Morgan as something she wanted to escape, and she would immediately respond with her flight behavior.

A dog's sense of smell is so much more acute than anything we can comprehend. Dogs can follow the scent of a track which is day's old. They can identify illicit drugs which have been surrounded with items to disguise their odor. It is suggested some dogs have the ability to identify cancerous tumors in humans that medical testing equipment cannot recognize. Such a profound sense of smell means the average dog can smell fear in humans. They can smell adrenaline in our blood stream, or a variety of other chemicals our bodies produce. Dogs have the ability to size up situations simply by the smells they are able to process.

When a dog enters a room of humans, they are able to assess which person is confident, which is scared, or who they can trust. If a dog can identify all of this information about humans they meet, we know they process even more information about other dogs.

This is why dogs can identify pack leaders, as well as their position in a pack based on the sense of smell. We all give off a variety of odors which vary based on our moods and feelings. I have found over the years of working with dogs, a dog may be attracted to specific humans, yet avoid other people. This is usually a dog-specific response unique to select humans. There are also humans who provoke a hostile response by a wide group of dogs, simply from the odor these individuals are emitting.

We also know humans smell different when they smile than when they frown and such a change in odor occurs in a split second. As quickly as a person's facial expression changes, so, too, does the odor their body emits. Such changes seem trivial to humans but they are strong signals to dogs. On many occasions I have observed the change in a dog's performance from perky and attentive to tentative and slow, when its teammate handler's facial expression and body language went from smiling and confident to disappointed and frustrated. When working with dogs it is important to realize how much information they are processing about their surroundings based on smell.

It took me a while to figure out the slightest change in my emotion produced profound reaction by Morgan. Once I understood the power of my emotional swings I began to understand the reactions of the dogs in our pack. Confident dogs show little reaction to the mood swings of humans around them. In contrast, those dogs lacking confidence have the most dramatic reaction to the mood swings of others. For example, if I was watching a football game on television and my team fumbled the ball, causing frustration and/or disappointment, the less confident dogs in our pack would disappear from the room and find a place as far away from me as possible. In contrast, when I had such an eruption of frustration, the confident dogs would remain right where they had been all along. I am sure the confident dogs were thinking crazy emotional human. Morgan was very sensitive to my moods.

In contrast, Liz and Julie (see earlier chapters) were very confident, so any change in my mood produced little reaction from them. In Liz and Julie's minds, they probably just recognized it for what it was – a human acting like a human with goofy emotions. Because they were so confident, my emotions had little effect on them or on how they reacted.

To get the best out of Morgan, I had to keep my emotions positive. This meant I needed to maintain a consistent positive attitude. Emotions are hard to control, because they are unplanned reactions. Most of my co-workers at the jobs I had had throughout life referred to me as intense. Since I had been an intense person, this was a good experience for me. Now I had to change my attitude to produce the desired behavior from Morgan. I had to learn to laugh at myself and my mistakes. With other dogs I have trained, I always treated the situation very serious, as disciplined work. With Morgan, training and showing had to become more like play. It wasn't the activity of training had changed; it was my attitude about it had to change. I had always been serious about training my dogs. In fact, I had always been serious about most everything I did.

I had to learn to laugh more, smile more, and talk in a happy higher pitched voice. What I learned is higher pitched voices sound happier than lower, deeper pitched voices, which sound serious or even angry. Due to the lower pitch, male voices tend to sound more serious and more frightening than do women's voices. When women react in anger, their voices are lower pitch. My first step to maximizing training success with Morgan was getting control of my emotions, reactions, and attitude so my demeanor stayed consistent, confident, and positive. If I stayed confident and consistent with Morgan, she then mirrored the same attitude. Under these conditions, Morgan was a great student who learned quickly and enjoyed working.

We quickly earned the first level of obedience title called Novice, earning three first place ribbons. Morgan was great, we worked well when we were together, but what would happen when I was not with her?

Dogs like to follow a confident leader.

One of the exercises at the next level of obedience called the Open level is a group out of sight sit and down. Out of sight sits and downs means a group of dogs competing in this class are lined up next to each other about 4 feet apart along one side of the show ring. After the dogs are lined up, the judge instructs the handlers to take off the dog's leashes and place them behind the sitting dogs. Next, the handlers are instructed to leave the ring, going out of sight for three minutes.

The second part of the exercise goes through the same steps except the dogs are left on a down stay and the handlers stay out of sight for five minutes.

Leaving Morgan alone in a dog show obedience ring with eight other dogs and no human handler was very scary for her. Practicing this exercise in a familiar environment produced minimal success. As soon as I disappeared from sight, Morgan wasted no time, in flight, to find me. She had learned and could correctly perform all of the other exercises in both Open and the highest level, Utility, because I was with her. But when her security blanket, me, disappeared, she went into her fear response, flight. Due to her fear of being left behind, out of sight sit and down exercise, was not going to be easy to train.

Knowing a skill does not result in performing that skill with success. Confidence is what separates those who achieve greatness and those who avoid a challenge.

Morgan was never going to have the confidence of Heidi, Julie, or Liz but she should be able to learn how to handle the stress of being alone for eight minutes in a dog show ring. As is the case when learning any new skill, the learning needs to be broken into small steps. Humans, as well as dogs, learn best when it is fed to them in small increments.

How do you eat an elephant; one bite at a time.

I created a detailed training plan. We started training in locations familiar to Morgan, so she could feel comfortable. By placing her in familiar locations she would feel safe. We worked in environments which were predictable, where nothing surprising or unexpected would occur. I wanted to build her confidence. Placing her on sit stays in places where she would not feel stress, such as in our house and leaving her for just seconds meant she began building her confidence that nothing bad would happen.

I would only leave Morgan alone for just short periods of time. We continued to train in the same locations, keeping everything as familiar as possible. When Morgan showed signs she could handle sitting alone in a familiar environment for a longer period of time, then I began to add dogs sitting next to her. The dogs I placed next to her initially were dogs she knew from her own pack and felt safe around.

The first dog to sit near Morgan was about 8 feet away; twice the distance she would experience in a competition setting. Once she was comfortable with one dog sitting next to her, I added a second dog, then a third dog – all of which were dogs Morgan had spent time with, and trusted. Many of these training experiences took place around our house and initially, the dogs sitting next to Morgan were her packmates. With each small step of success, Morgan gained a little bit more confidence. So, I gradually increased the length of time that I was out of sight, and then introduced her to a new environment.

168

I would only add one of these new challenges to a training session at a time.

Little successes motivate.
BIG failures De-Motivate.

Since Morgan was so lacking in confidence, it was critical for her to feel a lot of little successes. She was never going to be a naturally confident dog, but she could learn to be more confident by keeping her environment as consistent as possible and by preparing her for unexpected situations. This is called proofing.

Proofing means creating situations which normally will not occur, but when on the rarest of circumstances occurs, the unexpected does not cause panic and stress resulting in a major failure. So as Morgan gained confidence to perform this exercise, it was important to proof her with a variety of minor distractions, such as noises, smell's, or items that would be visually of interest. I would drop items that would make loud noises, blow horns, barking dogs, squeaky dog toys, or the sound of a noisy air conditioning fan. Bring aromatic foods into the training location are a great distraction. Since Morgan really like chasing tennis balls, I would have someone bounce a tennis ball or roll it across the room.

Each distraction was introduced in small increments, which I felt she could cope with. I never wanted to present Morgan with too much to think about. I worked toward taking Morgan into a new environment and placing her next to dogs she had never been introduced to before. She was instructed to sit for three minutes while I was out of sight, multiple times every week for months, before I felt she had the confidence to enter a competitive trial. It ultimately took 18 months before I felt Morgan had developed the confidence to handle a show environment with me out of sight.

Morgan had gained enough confidence to perform the out of sight exercises perfectly at enough trials to earn the desired titles. But,

169

due to her overall lack of confidence, Morgan never enjoyed competing at dog shows or even walking into a dog show environment, we stopped showing.

I continued training Morgan because she enjoyed the learning experience. Instead of attending competitive events, we played more games such as dock diving, chasing tennis balls, and field work just for the fun. Morgan lived out her life in our pack, traveling with me doing a lot of fun things in many fun locations.

CLARK

Field sales people work geographic territories selling products for the companies they represent. Most field sales reps work out of their automobile, driving from customer to customer presenting their companies' products.

Field sales people have managers who typically spend several days every month riding with them in their territories. Most often, these sales manager's visits take place over two consecutive days. For the sales person, these are stressful days – having your boss overseeing your every action. Most sales managers use these visits to insure sales people are correctly, and properly following company policies. Sales managers like to spend time on these visits reviewing the sales person's call reports, paper work, expense reports, and generally reinforcing the sales person is doing things "the company way."

Some sales managers become managers for the ego of the promotion, and then they realize how much they miss selling. So when they ride with their sales people they want to do all of the selling. Others have the Superman complex – they feel a need to jump into situations as if they are saving the day. In most of these cases, the participation of the sales manager does more harm than good with customer relations.

In contrast, I had a sales manager named Clark. When Clark rode with me it was a different experience than with any other sales managers I'd previously worked with. When Clark spent time working with his sales people, he was focused on doing investigative work – to learn more about competing company's sales people.

For example, on a typical sales call with other sales managers, the manager sits in on the sales presentation with the customer – as a third party overseeing the interchange between sales person and customer. The conversation revolves around collecting information on competing products the customer is using while presenting the feature and benefits of your product. These sales calls are usually uncomfortable for everyone, including the customer because they know the sales person is being evaluated on everything said.

With Clark, he would often opt out of meeting with the customer and instead sit in the waiting room to converse with the receptionist and office staff. He would ask questions about their favorite sales people. Clark understood the knowledge and influence office support staff has on any company's purchasing decisions. Clark wanted to know the preferred sales people who called on their office. Why did the office staff like particular sales representatives? He also knew the support staff could provide more accurate information about his own sales people than what he could learn by overseeing sales presentations. So, while I was speaking with the customer, Clark was asking questions of the customer's staff, such as the receptionist, office administrators, purchasing representatives. He not only asked about me but also about other sales people who visited their company.

Clark spent his time trying to identify the best sales person in every territory. He then kept files on those sales people who he had heard good things but worked for other companies. Then he contacted these respected sales people and set up one-on-one meetings –

171

usually over breakfast or lunch. Those that he liked and established a rapport, Clark would build an ongoing sustained relationship. This way when a sales rep in Clark's district was promoted, he already had the replacement to fill the vacant spot.

Most managers are reactive – only interviewing when they have an open position. Not Clark. He was always interviewing, finding talented people so he was prepared when a vacancy occurred.

Companies lose sales opportunities and revenue when territories are empty. The sales territories in Clark's district were always at the top in all sales categories to a degree, because he never had empty territories. Another reason was the sales people he hired were already good before he hired them, and then he made them better.

Another example of how Clark always wanted to surround himself with the best people, Clark was not the oldest member of his district; he had two sales reps that were in their sixties. Both of the older sales reps had distinguished careers in medical sales, including each having been in management roles with previous companies. Both were excellent sales people who had built long term professional relations with most of the prominent physicians in the area.

They had very loosely designated territories and responsibilities. Clark used these two individuals partly as an inner counsel for him to bounce ideas and thoughts, as well as, district leaders establishing the culture of our district because they had the respect of everyone in the district. Clark was not threatened by the experience, knowledge, or professional stature of either. Similarly the two older sales people recognized Clark as the Alpha, and appreciated the special role they played in the district.

Clark gave them unique assignments such as one of the two 60 years olds might call younger district members to provide advice; or at a meeting spend time with selected district members reviewing a selected topic; or contact a district member to spend a day riding together introducing the younger lesser experienced salesperson to key customers. Having one of these two distinguished individuals make an introduction to a high profile account was invaluable to the younger district member.

They both seemed to take a special interest in me, maybe because the older of the two was partly responsible for Clark hiring me. Or possibly since I was the youngest member of the district and needed the most help. In any case, I was very fortunate to receive such personal tutelage from both of these gentlemen at such an early stage of my career. The age difference was great enough either of them could have been my grandfather. Clark was very effective utilizing the talents and years of experience these two senior citizens brought to his district. Their mentoring of others allowed Clark the time to plan for the future using goal setting.

A goal without a plan is merely a dream.

Clark liked developing people and working to help them get promoted. He spent time finding the career goals for all of the people who worked for him. Then he would create plans to help each person achieve their goals. Clark was always thinking in the future, directing the success of his district by hiring the best people, creating a plan for their success, and coaching his sales team. When he was recognized for his continuous accomplishments, he always gave credit for success to the sales people. Clark spent his time preparing for the future. Clark had a vision of the big picture. He knew what he wanted his team to accomplish and prepared plans to accomplish his goals. Like playing chess, the great players don't make moves in reaction to their opponents. They make moves in preparation for future moves by both competitors – always thinking two moves ahead.

173

"I don't skate to the puck, I skate to where the puck is going."

Wayne Gretsky

We were never bored because Clark was always creating new challenges. He recognized the special talent each person had, and then gave assignments and recognition to maximize those strengths. He did not pit anyone against another, but rather created a cooperative competition. When done properly peer pressure can be a powerful tool to build a strong team motivating each member to work harder to keep up with team mates.

Peer Pressure is a Powerful Motivator.

For example, there were always several sales people in Clark's district with the goal of becoming a District Sales Manager. Those people were given the responsibility for planning, organizing and running the quarterly district sales meetings. There were other members of the district who wanted to work in the corporate office and they were given assignments providing them the opportunity to interface with people in corporate office.

Clark enjoyed teaching people in his district tasks involved in his job, and providing them the opportunities to perform those tasks, which in turn opened time for Clark to find new talent, train new skills and learn even newer skills. Clark understood the concept of proofing. As subordinates displayed confidence and consistency with previously learned assignments, Clark would slowly increase their responsibilities or interject unexpected obstacles testing the individual's ability to handle change.

Slow steps to learning and new responsibilities kept his staff motivated and feeling successful. Clark never referred to this practice as proofing, which was exactly what he was doing, creating new challenges in very small steps. All of these activities helped prepare his district members for their next jobs.

Yet others in the district liked sales and their job in sales, so Clark would find ways to reward these individuals with such things a Senior Sales Rep or Field Sales Trainer. He was always finding training opportunities for everyone in his district. By sharing his job responsibilities, it freed him to spend time planning for the future meetings with the people who could contribute to the success of his team. Helping his sales staff develop skills for a promotion, Clark had time to promote his staff to corporate positions.

By getting his subordinates promoted, he became a very powerful person in the organization. Clark was the reason those people had the opportunity to get promoted –In turn, those who had been given opportunities by Clark realized their responsibility to help others. Clark had been with the organization a long time and seemed to have hired half the company. With such a reputation, people wanted to work for Clark. Since so many of his former district sales people were in positions of influence throughout the organization, he had the inside track to getting future district sales members promoted.

This was a self-perpetuating process. The more people who got promoted, the more opportunities there were to get promoted. Because Clark was such a confident person, a true Alpha, he was not threatened getting members of his district promoted to positions above his in the formal organization. He relished in the opportunity to help others achieve their goals. Because he was a true Alpha, no matter how much success these former district members had, Clark remained their Alpha.

If you help others achieve their goals,
you will achieve your goals.

Although his title was district field sales manager, Clark was one of the most powerful and influential people in the entire organization. So many of the organization's vice presidents and department heads were from Clark's district, they talked with him weekly. The company's upper management, including the president, recognized the depth of respect Clark possessed, frequently consulting him before making important decisions. They also realized the influence he had in the organization and the impact his position on issues, would have on its success or failure in the organization. Clarks acceptance or belief in a policy went a long way as to how others would respond.

Clark's relationships stretched outside the organization as well. He'd earned the respect of customers. His bonds were so strong with many of these customers he had them trained to be on the lookout for potential sales people for him hire. Customers would make unsolicited recommendations to him regarding future hires.

His district was a well-tuned machine, which from the outside gave the appearance Clark was lucky to have everyone doing his work and making his life easy.

Luck is when Preparation meets Opportunity

In reality, Clark had spent years scouting talented people and then helped them build their skills to achieve their individual goals. Clark was the Alpha, he had confidence, and had earned the respect of his district members. Regardless how often a member of the pack changed, the results didn't. It was a pack working together in the best interests of the whole. If I had a problem, I knew exactly which member of the district had the best skills to help me solve a specific issue.

176

Clark liked having sales people in his district promoted. He liked change, so he was constantly hiring new people to fill open sales territories.. Changing members of the district meant there were always fresh ideas coming into his district. Sales people in Clark's district did not fall into ruts or get bored because change was constant.

Whenever a new salesperson took over a sales territory, which had become open due to a promotion, the new sales person would find new customers, because everyone has their own unique skill set. Each newly hired salesperson discovered untapped opportunities. Even the greatest sales person is not capable of getting along with everyone, nor are they able to fully develop every account. Turnover is good for everyone.

Clark's true skill was his ability to put other's needs in front of his own.

Clark could accomplish this success because he understood the goals and aspirations of each individual in his pack and he worked individually with each one creating a plan to achieve those goals. Clark created strategic plans for his district built around the individual development goals of his district members. He used his strategic plans and the plans established by each district member to help control his environment. Don't get me wrong, Clark dealt with unexpected daily problems, but they were a minor component of our daily routine, not the main course.

Firehouse Management

Managers in most companies spend their time reacting to their work environment of unexpected daily problems, unplanned requests, and emergency conference calls created by other people. These are the activities of those who let their surrounding world control their life, rather than the opposite. These are the behavior exhibited by people whose work practice revolves around the use of firehouse management. Managers who fill their days busily running around putting out fires are referred to as firehouse managers. Their lack of goals, plans, team building and training has them always looking busy and stressed while never making progress, simply treading water. They spend every day doing the same thing over and over, simply responding to their environment rather taking charge of and controlling their environment. These people are living in the world of firehouse management, letting others control their life. They lack a vision to create goals, which are used to develop plans needed to move their organization forward.

**If you don't know where you are going,
any road will get you there.**

This is where goals are established. What do you want to accomplish? Then what is the best vehicle to get to that destination? Leaders create a vision; that becomes the organizations mission. This information is then used to formulating organization goals; these goals are then used to create plans. Each of these plans is then broken down by departments for organization members to use in their daily activities. This is what separates packs that are excelling, compared to those who merely exist, continually repeating unproductive behavior.

GOALS

Most people spend more time making a shopping list than they do making life goals. It is estimated, less than 8 percent of the entire US population has goals. Those who do have goals are more likely to get things done, because they have a plan. And, people with a plan use their time wisely.

Goals are critical to success. Successful people first make long-term goals called "strategic planning". Their planning starts with a vision, such as where they want to be 10 years from now. From that vision, they establish specific long-term goals, then work backward from where they want to be to where they need to start. Each long term goal need to be broken down into yearly components until they can bring their focus to today's activities.

- Long-term goals should be 5-10 years in the future.
- Mid-range goals are 1-5 years in the future.
- Short-term goals are 3 months to 1 year from now.
- Immediate goals are less than 3 months from now.
- Daily is what you will do today to get closer to your long-term goal.

Working with this outline, it is important to begin planning from the furthest point out, or your long-term goals.

Long-term goals (5-10 years
Where do you want to be in 5-10 years in each of the below categories?

Career: Where do you want your career to be? What job do you want in 5-10 years? What job title do you want to have in 5-10 years? What does the organization you are working in 5-10 years look and act like?

Social: Who will be your friends in 5-10 years? What will be your social activities?

Mental: What books, classes, training, and/or education will you need over the next 5-10 years to achieve your long term goal? What certifications, degrees, or licenses do you want to earn in the next 5-10 years?

Spiritual: What will your beliefs be in 5-10 years to achieve your long term goal?

Physical: What will your health be in 5-10 years and what will you do to get there? Do you want to learn to downhill ski, learn martial arts, scuba dive in Hawaii, play racquetball twice per week, compete in a marathon or other challenge.

Financial: What will be your income in 5-10 years? How much money will you need? What investment will you have? What will your house look like? How much insurance will you need? What will you own or owe money on?

Family: What will your family look like in 5-10 years? Number of children, etc.? What schools will your children will attend? How much will they need for college, trade school, weddings, etc?

Mid-range goals (1-5 years)
Next, you need to take each of the seven categories above and break them down into a more detailed plan, what needs to be accomplished in 1-5 years from this date.

Short-term goals (3-12 months)
After you have completed your mid-range goals for each category then you need to take the categories and develop a detailed short-term plan for each.

Immediate Goals (less than 3 months)
Then you need to analyze each of your short-term goals for each category and develop an immediate plan for each. What do you need to accomplish within the next year to move you toward your ultimate long-term goals?

Daily (today)

Are your daily activities aligned with your long term goals? Your daily activities should in some way, every day, move you closer to your long term goals. Immediate too long term goals should be considered when planning daily goals.

What you think about is what you become.

Goals need to be broken into small steps, the smaller the better. It is easier to create training for small steps than huge strides. Small steps are easier to evaluate for progress. And by assessing the progress of small steps, it allows constant road markers of success. If participants are traveling on the prescribed training route, with short interval check points, it is easier to ensure they are on the correct course. In contrast, if the steps are huge strides with large lengths of time expiring between check points, then training can be way off course before it is recognized and corrections made. It also takes a lot less time and work to make small detours on the course than to get so far down the wrong path you have to design a whole new plan.

Goals broken into small easy-to-digest components are more rewarding to participants. The feeling of success is a valuable motivator.

Little successes = Motivation

BIG failures = De-Motivation

Lastly, when establishing goals, people need to have a deadline for completion. This should include frequent check points to insure you are on the correct road for success. Each check point needs to have deadlines for completion. What separate those who accomplish goals from those who don't are the words the two groups of people use.

Those who accomplish goals use words like "I **will** accomplish my goal on this given date." Those who do not accomplish goals use words like "one of these days I am going to accomplish my goal."

I have known many people who spend their lives saying, "one of these days I am going to Hawaii". One of these days never arrives because they have not committed themselves to a specific time and or date.

Successful goal begins with: "I will …
Unsuccessful goal begins with: "Someday I hope to …"
Someday never gets here.

All goals and their plans need to be documented in writing. If they are not in writing, they lack commitment. Weekly goals also need to be reviewed to understand your accomplishments the past week and assign tasks for the up-coming week.

If you don't measure it; you can't manage it.

Leaders have goals, for not only themselves, but also for the people they are responsible for leading. They use those goals to create a vision for pack members to rally around and use them as a direction toward which to move. Having a vision for the pack to move toward is very important.

Finish Line phenomenon

Goals function as a target to aim our efforts. When a goal target has been established, the brain focuses its efforts to hit exactly the goals place, time, and value. Achieving that specific accomplishment is motivating and important toward keeping the person who set the goal on the most efficient path to success. This is what makes goal setting such a useful motivational tool.

Unfortunately, most people strive to hit their goal, but not surpass the goals they set for themselves, which known as the finish line phenomenon. Most people seldom exceed the goals they set for themselves or are set for them. Once they have reached their goal they reduce their momentum. The goal functions more of a finish line than a success marker on a much greater path. As a goal becomes closer to completion people monitor their efforts so as to meet the goal rather than supersede it. Leaders have to pay close attention to progress toward organization goals insuring staff not only receives constant feedback on progress but also keep goals challenging.

It is useful to provide multiple goals each with increasing difficulty and higher reward for accomplishment to continue building momentum, and not experience the finish line phenomenon.

Proofing

To reduce the chances of failure and improve the opportunity for success, at a particular activity, it is helpful to repeatedly practice or proof the exercise. Proofing is practicing a particular exercise under stressful or challenging conditions to build confidence. For example sports teams practicing with loud blaring sound to simulate game day crowd noise. Or a domed football team practices passing, catching, carrying footballs soaked in ice water to simulate playing out doors in January. Those are some of the examples of how sports teams proof to build confidence.

In the dog world, proofing involves a practice session in which trained exercises are done while distractions are occurring for both dog and handler. This can include loud or unusual noises. Proofing can involve practicing exercises having to work around dishes of dog food on the floor; or the dog's favorite toys on the floor.

Proofing prepares participants for the unexpected, reducing the chance of failure when the unanticipated occurs, because team mates are prepared when surprises occur. These are just some examples of trainable activities to reduce mistakes and build confidence. Feeling prepared improves the chances for success leading to improving confidence.

Strategic vs Tactical

Monthly goals need to be revised based on the past month's accomplishments. This is when the tactical adjustments come into play. Because the environment is always changing, alterations called tactical plans need to occur to compensate for such changes. The difference between strategic plans and tactical plans is the difference between seeing the big picture – the strategic plan – and the individual paint strokes – the tactical plan – which completes the painting.

A great example to illustrate these two concepts is maneuvering a sailboat across a lake against the wind. The strategic plan is to leave port on the south side of the lake and to arrive at a specific location on the opposite or north side of the lake. But, the wind is blowing from north to south, the opposite of the direction you wish to travel. Since your only source of power are the sails, you must tack, which is the technical term given to a series of an east to west, then east again, alternating zig-zag pivoting maneuvers. Tacking is a time-consuming, calculated pattern of course changes, which will ultimately get you to your desired destination.

In this example, your strategic plan is to leave the south lake port to arrive at the north side of the lake port. But as the wind changes in velocity and direction, the sailboat captain must frequently change the direction of the tacks, and the frequency of the alternating zig-zag course pivots from east to west to east. Such environment changes will influence the time required to travel across the lake and the ultimate time of arrival.

184

You can't control the direction of the wind, but you can adjust the sails to ultimately reach the destination, which is the tactical plan. The strategic goal is to get from the south port to the north port side of the lake. The tactical plan is to take as many tacks as necessary to cross the lake and reach the other side of the lake.

Strategic plans are designed to achieve the ultimate goal based on the knowledge at the onset; tactical plans are adjustments made to the strategic plan as the environment changes over time.

Goals need to be few in number and frequent in review.

If you don't do something that makes you uncomfortable every day, you really aren't living.

Chapter Nine

PARKER

Approximately one year-old a Golden Retriever mix came to us as a foster from the Golden Retriever Rescue. He was a high energy, intelligent, athletic, 65-pound playful dog which would have us laughing at his antics one minute, and angry at his destructive behavior minutes later. His intelligence made him a fun dog to train – as long as he was receiving mentally-stimulating direction. But when he was bored or out-thinking the humans around him, he would get himself into trouble.

We fostered Parker before the availability of DNA testing, so we never really knew what his mix was -- but his instinctive behavior was to herd, often nipping at people's heels. Parker had the alert drive of a Border Collie, which his perky ears might suggest. Based on his physical appearance he had the body shape of a Labrador Retriever or Golden Retriever. All three of these breeds are typically smart, some more biddable than others. His brain was always thinking and calculating way ahead of the rest of the world. He did not follow directions just for the sake of conforming to routine. Parker seemed to need a reason for why he was asked to do things. What's in it for me might be a good way to explain how he viewed the world.

As with every dog entering our pack, the dynamics and relationship of the entire pack membership changes. Some dogs move up the ladder; others move down. This change in pack status also impacts the relationships between all pack members. Parker came into a pack of all female retrievers. Simply by default, he entered the pack as the alpha male of the dogs. A relationship with Liz, a red-headed Golden Retriever rescue, was quickly established. They were the two alphas and both very similar in energy and intelligences.

I believe they were the two most intelligent members of the pack. If they were not provided with proper leadership there was a potential of getting into trouble. Both would lead if they did not have a good reason to follow the humans in the pack. They were the canine leaders of this pack, but because our pack also included two humans Bonnie and I who for sanity sake needed to be the leaders. Dogs like humans require leadership to be earned, so Bonnie and I had to prove ourselves to these two. Parker learned quickly and retained what he had learned. He was also fearless, not afraid to try any new challenge.

Every dog coming into our pack is exposed to obedience training. We start with the five basic fundamental skills: sit, stay, down, come and heel. Parker quickly learned both the verbal and visual cues to perform each of these five exercises. An average dog can learn and understand about 200 words, above average dog is capable of properly responding to 400 words, a smart dog is able to understand and appropriately respond to 800 words, and a very smart dog understands and properly reacts to 1,200 words. Parker was definitely at the upper end of this scale. With a dog as smart and athletic as Parker, he had a lot of potential to learn agility and obedience exercises.

But before a dog can learn how to jump over obstacles, run through tunnels, climb A-frames, maneuver weave poles, and perform other agility exercises, they need to understand and properly respond to obedience commands. So, after Parker learned fundamental obedience he was ready for agility training. As with our experience training obedience skills, Parker quickly learned to master the agility obstacles with enthusiasm.

Learning the foundation skills is simply that – the most elementary exercises, which are then used to learn further skills. If you want to write a thesis, one must first learn to spell, which is where we found ourselves with Parker. Similar to teaching any skill, most instructors use repetitive routines. With most dogs, such routines are important to developing confidence and consistency. Training sessions consists of repeating the same exercises until the instructor feels the student had mastered the skills, before attempting the next level. Most trainers have their favorite training exercises, which become a very routine pattern. It is easy to become a creature of habit and repeat the same activities every session. But this wouldn't work with a dog like Parker, who became bored with training if I continued using the same exercises over and over.

If your only tool is a hammer; all of your problems look like nails.

To keep Parker engaged, the training needed to be different and challenging. This meant the trainer needed to become very creative with training exercises and sessions. Changing the environment, location, surroundings was one way to keep each experience interesting. It is also important the exercises look different to the dog. This is what makes a trainer better because they are forced out of their comfort zone. Parker challenged us to look at new training exercises and new ways of presenting information. He enjoyed learning when he was challenge to think and build on what he had previously learned.

189

For me to have a successful transfer of information with Parker, required the ability to communicate with each other. Parker had to understand what I was trying to teach and I had to properly interpret when he was bored, confused, or understanding what I was trying to teach.

To maintain the respect and attention of my pupil I was constantly on the lookout for new training exercises, either of my own creation or what I could copy from other trainers. I could not fall into predictable training routines or he would get bored. So, change was an important function of motivation and interest. Parker made me a better trainer, because he forced me to think differently. I could not get into habits or ruts.

To keep a dog or person's interest; you have to be more interesting than any other option.

About the time Parker was ready to begin entering dog show performance trials the perfect person came along interested to adopt him. It took a special person to adopt Parker, someone who could laugh at his silliness and still command Parkers respect. In addition, the right companion for Parker had to be someone who would provide an environment for daily physical activity. His new teammate was a recently widowed, 6'-4"retired police officer, who had a house on a lake and drove an SUV, they just looked like they fit together. Since his adoption, Parker receives daily swimming in the lake, walks and tennis ball retrieve. His new human pack mate has provided us with frequent communication on Parker development, which sounds like a great life. In those communications Parker is often referred to as a chick magnet.

FRANK

Frank grew up in a family-owned business. He worked in the business for his father while in high school, college and then ultimately purchased the business from his parents. Frank's parents had owned and run their family business most of their lives. When Frank took over, there were eight employees working out of one location. His parents had left him with a well-established company in their life long community. This was a company built on the commitment to deliver personal service and quality products. Out of their one location with eight employees they had always provided customers with down home family-owned business type of care.

But Frank was not like his parents, he had a history of being the company prankster. Frank liked to joke with co-workers, and he always had a smile on his face. Under Frank's leadership, the company changed in personality from the serious attitude his parents had built to a bit looser work environment where practical jokes were part of a normal day. Frank also inherited several employees who had more years with the organization than he had. They also possessed different skills than Frank.

Although they had more years with the company and different skill sets, these employees were not viewed as a threat, but embraced by Frank as valuable company assets. And like Frank, some of these long-term employees were participants in the pranks and practical jokes. The company experienced a refreshing change in philosophy and direction. Frank added fun to the work place and he was very effective at weaving fun into the responsibilities of making the business successful.

Frank was very skilled at communicating with employees his goals and expectations for both the organization, as well as, each employee. For example, Frank was very effective getting the involvement and commitment of his staff as to how he wanted to expand the geographic area served, number of locations, scope of services, and staff. Based on the vision he created and the dedication of his employees, over the next 20 years, Frank grew the company to over 75 employees working out of nine locations.

Organizations take on the personality of it leader.

One of the first changes Frank introduced to his staff was an annual company meeting. These once a year meetings took place on a Saturday so as to not take away from the five-day, 40-hour work week service their customers were accustomed to receiving. Employees were properly compensated for the Saturday they spent attending a work function. These are not your typical boring company meetings, instead the learning is bundled with fun and entertainment. In addition, each year's meeting provides great food at breakfast and lunch. The days schedule is well organized with a meeting theme and meeting goals, they are a lot of fun with laughter at their core. The meeting themes changed every year and are kept a secret from the employees until the day of the meeting. The meeting themes are elaborate in design requiring a great deal of organization and detail. All of the training manuals, presentation, posters, signs, and registration reflected the theme topic. A great deal of effort is spent on room decorations, name badges, meals, presentations, dress code, etc.

These annual meetings are not only a lot of fun, more importantly; they were a vital forum for education and team building. Frank brings in the company's banker, insurance provider and other organizations providing company employee benefits and other services. During these meetings employees learn about their current benefits and services they receive as a component of their employment. The benefits offered to Franks employees are some of the best I have seen from any size organization. Frank truly cares about his employees and takes very good care of them. He understands the importance of hiring excellent people; offering the best benefits, providing pertinent training and education. During the program, employees are required to answer questions about company policies and programs; correct answers are compensated with incentives and rewards.

> **All business is reduced to three things**
> **people, products and profit,**
> **unless you have a great team,**
> **you can't do much with the other two.**
>
> **Lee Iacocca**

As the company grew in employees so, too, did the importance of these annual meetings. Frank's annual company meeting felt more like a family reunion than a company function. The company was built on trust, co-operation and respect. Observing the employees at these functions was like watching friends gather for party. Laughter is always a common component.

This was not Frank's company and these are not his subordinates, to him they were his family. He knew all their names, their children's and spouse's names, and their favorite activities.

One of the most unique events at every year's meeting, Frank provide the oldest tenured employee 15 minutes in front of the entire company to speak on any topic. This person didn't have to tell Frank, or anyone else in the company, in advance, what the topic would be. The senior employee is one of Frank's primary co-pranksters. He is one of the company's most jovial employees. He is a father figure to some, grandfather to others, and best friend to many, loved by both coworkers and customers. The relationship between the two men is more like brothers than employer and employee.

Because the senior employee, is known as a prankster and jokester, there was no telling what might come out of his mouth.

Uncensored and live with a microphone in hand, it could be a stand-up comedy routine or chaos.

This oldest tenured employee grew up in a small rural town and never completed high school. Without a formal education he had learning his occupation through years of on-the-job training. Spending his life overcoming many challenges he had risen to the position as head of a department in Franks company.

This annual presentation had become a very popular event due to the laughter he could produce. At this particular meeting he stepped to the podium and introduced his topic: "The Storm". Oh boy, this should be good. It had all the makings of a big complaint session.

He began his presentation talking about the bell-shaped curve which every product or business experiences. It begins at the lower left-hand corner of the graph with a line moving left to right, slowly sloping curve, ever so slightly upward. He goes on stating, this is referred to as the INFANCY stage of the curve. As the slope continues to the right, the slope makes an aggressive angle upward, which he explained, is the GROWTH stage. As the bell-shaped curve begins to levels off to the point of being flat and starts to curve downward, this is the MATURE stage. Lastly, on the far right side of the graph is a sharp downward slope reflecting a drastic drop in sales, which is referred to as the DECLINING stage.

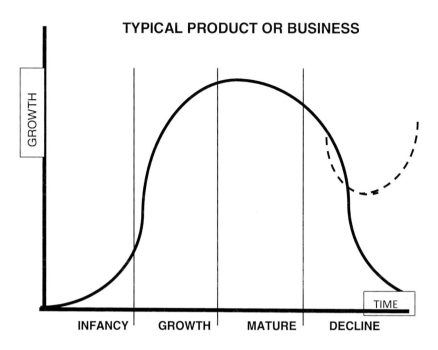

TYPICAL PRODUCT OR BUSINESS

GROWTH

TIME

INFANCY | GROWTH | MATURE | DECLINE

The employee continued to explain how in most organizations, change does not take place until revenue and profits begin to move from the mature stage into the declining stage. At this point, the company's momentum is downward and moving fast into a deeper and deeper decline, which makes it difficult to reverse the direction. Unfortunately, it is not until companies reach this stage when management begins to get interested to change their practices.

Reviewing again the graph and providing even greater detail he explained how in the Infancy stage, companies experience a lot of excitement, new ideas and many changes in procedures. There is no routine to the day. Everything is a little chaotic while people have to adjust and adapt to what is expected. Roles are not clearly defined. Everyone has to continuously think throughout the day to achieve the organization's desired goals. In the Growth stage, the work environment is similar to the infancy stage, except roles, rules and procedures are becoming more defined. Due to the rapid growth, everyone is busy and working hard. Because of the fast pace, staff is never really able to relax, always busy working, trying to keep up. But as time progresses and the company begins to move from the growth stage to the mature stage, habits and routines begin to develop. In most organization this is when employees get into ruts, the job becomes predictable, more time is spent drinking coffee and gossiping. The job is now becoming less exciting, more routine and possibly boring. As a result, productivity drops off. So too does the creativity of employees as they become comfortable with daily habits.

This is not the case for Frank, before boring and complacency can occur in our organization; Frank introduces "The Storm." Before employees can get comfortable with their jobs, before habits and routines develop into ruts, which is a common trait of most companies in the mature stage, Frank introduces "The Storm." So, what is The Storm? It's defined as change. Any change. Frank will change the computer system. Frank will change staff from one location to another. Frank will change the building appearance either with furniture, paint or by moving walls. He will change the dress code or company procedures. Frank will change something causing the staff to think a little different. These changes are accompanied with training and information to explain the changes taking place.

He won't let his employees settle into ruts. There is no auto-pilot in his company. He wants employees to always be on their toes, constantly thinking, seeing things a little differently, excited to come to work. All of these changes are intermixed with fun, jokes and pranks, so it keeps everyone alert. This keeps people excited about their jobs. Which is why Frank's company keeps growing ... The Storm.

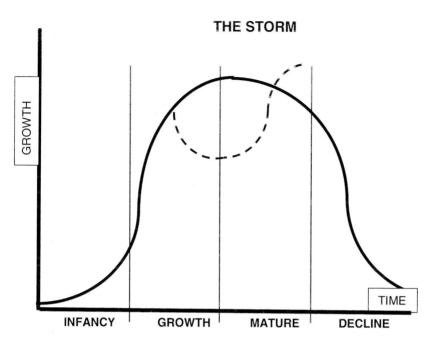

THE STORM

GROWTH

TIME

INFANCY | GROWTH | MATURE | DECLINE

To run a company with changes similar to The Storm, there needs to be a great amount of communication. Frequent changing of things such as staffing or computer billing systems, or procedures requires dependable communications. Change is good, but without a clear, clean, systems of communication such changes will produce problems. Frank had mastered the skill of both.

If you are not having fun you are doing it wrong.

Since organizations take on the personality of their leadership, Frank's staff not only embraces change; many of the changes instituted by Frank were recommendations or comments made by his employees. Frank is a good listener. He spends a lot of time talking with his employees, during when he hears comments of things employees believe would make their jobs better he listens and then he institutes The Storm.

Change

The world is in constant change. People are either moving ahead or falling behind, there is no such thing as standing still. Those who embrace the status quo and resist change will quickly become the past. Those who understand change, as difficult as it is, can produce fun, and it makes us more interesting. Change requires learning, so people who learn new things are changing. People who incorporate change in their lives are far more interesting to talk with. They have new ideas and are energetic about their lives.

If you are not challenging yourself with creative ideas and new experiences, it becomes easy to fall into habits and routines, making people boring and predictable. Great leaders have the responsibility for keeping pack members engaged and learning. New ideas create growth.

Hawthorne Effect

In 1924, the United States was in the midst of amazing manufacturing growth. Henry Ford's assembly line manufacturing technique was being applied to many companies. Bell Telephone was among those companies to put assembly line practice into their facilities. This included the Western Electric factory in Cicero, Illinois referred to as Hawthorne Works. The factory was spread over 100 acres and employed over 40,000 people. The employment policies at the Western Electric factory were also very progressive for that era – offering one week vacation after five years of constant employment, as well as a pension program. This led to a first of its kind research study done in a cooperative effort between the National Academy of Science, The National Research Council, The Rockefeller Foundation and Harvard Business School to investigate worker productivity.

Hawthorne Works commissioned a study to investigate methods of increasing worker productivity. The first step was to study the effect of luminescence (lighting) on worker's motivation. The researchers selected specific areas of the factory where lighting could be controlled and contained. They made slight changes to the lighting intensity in selected factory locations, and then studied the reaction of the workers in those areas. Researchers wanted to know if work area luminescence would have any influence on employee production and output. Some work place areas received a slightly brighter lighting and others slightly dimmer. The researchers then closely tracked production output in each of these work areas. Those work areas which had changes in luminescence intensity experienced increases in production based on the number of units produced. Each of the luminescent changes were sustained and observed for several weeks.

Next, researchers made changes in the cleanliness of work areas. They cleared the floor areas of any obstacles in selected work areas. Lastly, they relocated the work area layout. With each of these changes came an increase in employee productivity, compared to pre-intervention data, as defined by the amount of finished product produced. Employee production increased with each intervention presented to workers. For example, regardless of whether the luminescent was brighter or dimmer, production increased. In fact, there was no significant difference in production improvement if the lighting was brighter or dimmer, but with each change came an increase in production.

The first studies were so successful additional new interventions were created to expand on what had been learned. In 1927, the lead researchers produced another study providing a variety of work schedules to determine what hours worked would motivate workers to produce the most telephone relays. Six female workers, who manufactured telephone relays, were placed in a room separate from other telephone relay assembly workers. The six women worked in the same room together, but each worked individually, assembling telephone relays. Each of the completed relays was dropped through a chute which was then mechanically counted and recorded. An hourly and daily record of completed relays was kept for each worker.

The first intervention placed on the six test subjects involved giving them two five-minute breaks, one in the morning the other in the afternoon, and their production exceeded the output of other workers. This work schedule was maintained for several weeks. Then the two breaks were expanded to 10 minutes each, and once again production increased. This work schedule was also maintained for several weeks. Next four more breaks were added, making it a total of six five-minute work breaks/per day, the production of relays, by all six women declined. As with the past two interventions, the schedule was maintained for several weeks. The work schedules were then returned to the original design; this too caused an increase in production.

A new intervention was added to the study, food was now provided during the breaks, this caused an increase in the number of telephone relays manufactured by each worker. This work schedule also continued for several weeks to insure the intervention had a lasting effect.

A third work schedule intervention was next created, shortening the work days. By shortening the work day by 30 minutes output increased. After several weeks, the work day was shortened again by another 30 minutes, the output by hour went up, but the total daily output was less than it had been prior to the shortening of the day by another 30 minutes. After several weeks the work schedule went back to the first 30 minute shorter day schedule and output peaked.

Over the course of five years, the women worked in a room separate from other workers, under observation, having the number of telephone relays assembled output closely counted. During this five-year study, an overall increase in production by 30% was observed by the cumulative output of the six women. After all of the data had been accumulated and reviewed the researchers came to some interesting conclusions.

Researchers believed changes in the work place caused increased production.

Years later, when the study was re-analyzed and data more closely scrutinized some new thoughts resulted. First, the behavioral changes taking place in employees to increase productivity, but interventions only lasted, on average, eight weeks. Many of the interventions lasted less than eight weeks. Those interventions which stayed in effect for more than eight weeks found, that after eight weeks production slowly declined to pre-intervention levels. Environmental changes only had short-term effects on employee motivation. Sustaining increased production requires constant change which in itself becomes predictable and non-motivating. At the same time, change is motivating and is a valuable leadership tool, but must be used with discretion.

The work place interventions taking place during the original research were not blind studies, so all employees at Hawthorne Works knew there were researchers running studies of their behavior. The researchers were visible and often asked questions of workers. It is believed workers were more motivated by the interest they received from researchers than from the interventions. It was motivating and flattering for the workers to have researchers asking questions expressing interest in them as people.

The most powerful motivator for workers was the feeling leadership took an interest in them as individuals.

Many of the interventions with the six female assemblers, leading to increased telephone relay production, were changes which the study subjects had suggested. In contrast, the interventions which did not work to increase production were activities the women did not prefer, in fact, they even stated those preferences while interviewed by researchers. This was the case when breaks were expanded to 6 five-minute breaks, which resulted in a decline in production. The women had stated, such a work schedule was not their preference prior to initiation of the intervention and responded with their behavior.

From 1924 through 1932, researchers interviewed over 21,000 Hawthorne Works employees asking their opinions. Those interview results were used for future projects at the factory. Humans respond favorably when they are asked their opinions and are given active participation in controlling their jobs. These interviews may have provided more motivation to employees than any one specific intervention. Even more motivating is when a person's opinion is asked and their feedback is used. This provides workers with a sense of ownership for the intervention's success. If a worker provides a suggestion and then the suggestion is acted on, the worker has a feeling of responsibility to make the suggestion work.

Initially, researchers believed changes in the environment influenced workers productivity, which to some extent is true. This is what has come to be referred to as the Hawthorne Effect. But after years of reviewing not just the study and its interventions, but also the research techniques employed by researcher and employee interview involvement The Hawthorne Effect may only occur when there is useable feedback or a change in motivation.

The last study implemented at Hawthorne Works involved pay incentives on productivity. A group of 14 men manufacturing telephone switching equipment were financially incentivized by the number each produced. Production did not increase. Surveys of these men resulted in a prepared response which was not truly representative of the individual employee's feelings, but in reality the responses given were what the workers believed it was what the researchers wanted to hear. By this point in the study, workers were becoming suspicious of the researchers and created informal groups referred to as "cliques" (also known as informal organizational communication, see chapter four). These "cliques", began creating their own rules to control the researcher's behavior.

Researchers learned, if employees do not trust the formal leadership of an organization then the informal organization "clique" is more powerful an influence than incentives established by management. In 1924-1932, when the Hawthorne Works studies were being conducted the researchers did not understand the importance of cliques. Now, years later, we are able to understand the power impact of the informal organization.

If the rate of change outside of the organization is faster than the rate of change inside the organization; the end is near.

Change for the sake of change might have short term impact on productivity. But, for sustained growth, change needs to be the result of long term goals. When change is broken down into small stepping stones on the path of a long term goals, achieving success is much higher. This requires commitment by all of the people affected by change. It also necessitates participation of those involved in change to be instrumental in the planning of changes that are implemented. Which means listening to those most affected by change is a critical component toward insuring change will be implemented and not sabotaged.

It is not necessary to change; survival is not mandatory.

W. Edward Deming

<u>SEVEN STEPS TO STAGNATION</u>
1. We've never done it that way.
2. We're not ready for that.
3. We're doing all right without it.
4. We tried that once before.
5. It costs too much.
6. That is not our responsibility.
7. It just won't work.
8. You obviously don't understand; we are different.

You are correct the title says seven steps to stagnation yet the list includes eight. For years when giving my presentation on change I had listed the first seven. Audiences frequent respond to this list by saying, "Russ you obviously don't understand; we are different". Everyone believes they are unique, and their business situation is unlike any other. My experience is that basic business principles are true for all business.

Past Behavior predicts Future Behavior.

Chapter Ten

MEA

When we first met Mea she was estimated to be 4 years old. Mea is a shorthaired hound, mostly white with several brown spots. Based on her appearance she was referred to as a Treeing Walker Coon Hound, about 35 pounds and 20 inches at the withers. She has very expressive ears when interested or excited she cocks them up as if saluting. But when she's unsure they droop around her face hanging like wet withered leaves. Her svelte, taunt posture and facial features are very striking.

The reason for her coming to live with us was due to her unstable disposition. She had no tolerance for any excitement or stress; some might call her a very high strung dog. After she had lived with us just a short time it became clear earlier in her life she had been physically abused. She was edgy, fearful and reactive to every little change in her environment.

From the little we learned about her earlier years, Mea had a life of constant change. She lived through a revolving door of short stays at many homes. Each home had different rules. Each home had humans with their own unique expectations and temperaments. Due to the many bad encounters she experienced early in life, Mea developed a greeting pattern of lashing out first. When approached by a stranger, Mea's first instinct was to lunge at people and bite them to scare them away.

This same behavior was exhibited when she would see another dog, in particular, small dogs. Her life must have been filled with fear. This was learned behavior from early in her life; she could not take a chance on trusting anyone. Mea's defense mechanism to fear (fight, flight or freeze) was not to run away or hide from strangers, rather to attack. Somewhere in her early life, Mea found attacking first was effective at scaring away others who may be potentially harmful. Early in her life Mea found this type of aggressive behavior worked, scaring away someone worked the first time, so she tried it again and the second stranger was also scared away. Now she had proven to herself a pattern of success.

Mea had learned the behavior, if she attacked first, she would be safe.

When we agreed to be a foster home for Mea, we did not know much about her or her history. Most rescue dogs have little documented history of the dog's prior life or experiences.

Mea was delivered by a representative of the rescue organization who met us, the new foster family, for the dog exchange. By this time in her life Mea had established a greeting behavior of lunging forward with an open, teeth bearing, mouth. This was exactly the greeting we received. And, unlike a lot of dogs, she did not offer any warning such as a growl or snarl. Fortunately, we had experience meeting new fosters and had similar greetings, so when she lunged out I was able to react to avoid contact.

When greeting her new pack, Mea's behavior was predictable – even on leash she lunged out to bite first in an effort to scare away this pack of dogs. Mea probably had never been part of a pack. And we knew the experience of integrating her into the pack would be a challenge. Especially since trust was not a familiar experience. For the first several months, she was very distrustful of the other dogs especially when her learned behavior to lunge at other dogs to scare them away did not work. The pack was here before Mea arrived and they had a trusting confident relationship with each other. Mea's attempts to scare away these other dogs did not result in success.

There were several altercations between Mea and Morgan, a 65-pound Golden Retriever. I attribute this to two issues. First Morgan had spent her life as the pack Omega, bottom of the pack hierarchy, who usually resorted to flight when threatened, so aggressive behavior was unusual for her. The addition of Mea to the pack caused competition for the bottom spot with Morgan. These were two serious Omegas, both scared, but Mea was even more fearful than Morgan.

Resource Guarding

The second issue was resource guarding, and the resource Morgan wanted to guard was me. Morgan and I spent a lot of time together training and she had become rather protective of me. Morgan reacted to Mea as a threat to our relationship. After living in our pack for four years, Morgan liked her life and feared Mea was a threat. She had developed her place in the pack and she was concerned about this newcomer taking her place. She did not want Mea to intrude on her relationship with me, which is referred to as resource guarding. Resource guarding can involve items other than personal relationship, it can include food, toys, and other possessions.

Morgan had developed a strong trust and respect for both Bonnie and I, so when she was told not to fight, she followed orders and resisted her instinctual urge to physically nail Mea. Morgan allowed Mea to lunge at her face and not retaliate. Morgan had always been the scared bottom of the pack dog but through the years of working together she developed enough self-confidence not run at every threat. When Mea would try to intimidate Morgan, she would look Mea in the eyes with serious confidence. The frequency of Mea's lunges toward Morgan slowly declined as Morgan maintained her stoic restraint. They were never going to be best friends; all we wanted was for them to tolerate each other.

Mea's lunging and attacking was not limited to dogs and humans. She would also attempt to bite inanimate objects. Household items included the vacuum cleaner. When the vacuum cleaner came out of the closet, Mea would attack – charging, barking, and biting this, to her, was a scary object even before it was turned on. This was another indication she had been teased and tormented by a vacuum sometime earlier in her life. The true cause of this reaction was fear. Mea was trying to scare away this object which had, earlier in her life, caused her a great deal of stress.

In an effort to reduce the potential harm which might be inflicted by a lunging dog with open mouth and exposed teeth, we trained Mea to carry a dog toy. We taught her to retrieve and carry a rubber toy or other smooth dog toy when greeting others, this minimized the chance of a dog tooth-to-skin interface. When Mea would get excited, we would tell her to bring her toy. She would immediately seek out and display a toy in her mouth upon return. This behavior by Mea, would produce verbal praise and rewards from us, thus, reinforcing her behavior. The more she showed her toys the more rewards she got. To redirect the bad behavior, this was an important habit to teach and reinforce.

Even after establishing a safe, non-threatening relationship with her new pack, Mea still kept a distance. Always very wary of anyone around her, she would avoid being touched, petted or having any other contact from other humans or animals. Mea tolerated the people who she could not scare away, but avoided getting close. We treated Mea with respect, not fear, to build her confidence. When someone would make a move toward her, Mea would immediately expand the space between her and the aggressor. Even on those unique occasions when she allowed someone to pet her, within seconds she would show her teeth and mouth the hand which was petting her. Based on her behavior, peaceful, coexistence, with other dogs was a new experience.

Respect and trust is earned, it cannot be forced.

The options for Mea's future were unfortunately, very limited. She was either going to stay with us and we would have to keep very close control over her environment and minimize the chances of her biting another person or dog, or be euthanized. Early on, due to the number of infractions between her and the other members of our pack, euthanizing was becoming a very serious consideration. For the first two years Mea lived with us, it was a very real option, to protect us and the other members of our pack.

Mea may have been the smartest dog we have ever had as a member of our pack. She possessed excellent problem-solving skills. Mea could learn new words and obedience exercise very quickly. She could perform those exercises as long as her environment was consistent and safe. This is when we tried exposing her to a new challenge such as attending obedience classes as observers. Such classes consisted of about 6 to 9 dog and handler teams.

The classes we chose had well trained dogs, which are comfortable around other dogs. It became apparent very quickly Mea would target dogs she viewed as a threat or vulnerable. Targeting is when dogs focus their attention on another dog in a threatening manner. For humans targeting would be similar to a stare down. After a few such experiences, we abandoned the idea of socializing Mea with non-pack members.

Even after living with us for several months, Mea did not want to be touched, petted and especially not picked up. Any attempt to pet her resulted in her quickly scooting way from the human who had gotten too close.

We had a cleaning lady who visited our house every other week. She had access to the house on an occasional basis rather than a daily. It was a situation where there was no pattern to her appearances. During Mea's first controlled meeting with the cleaning lady, there weren't any signs of lunging or an aggressive reaction. For the next several visits, we continued the same controlled introduction process. From that time on when the cleaning lady would enter our house, Mea, with a waging tail, would search out a toy she could show off. Mea found a human she could trust. Was it the fact the cleaning lady had dogs of her own and was not afraid of Mea and acted with confidence around Mea? What we learned was once Mea met the cleaning lady and felt safe she could be trusted.

Once Mea found she could trust a human or dog she would happily greet an established friend with a waging tail and exuberance. This was proven many times with family, friends and their dogs. She greeted the friends with wagging tail and licks. For the first three years she lived with us, she did not want to be touched, petted, or receive any affection. Then, for whatever reason, she slowly began to pursue attention. Mea wanted to be petted. She wanted to receive affection. Her confidence had grown enough to allow her to put down the defenses and be open to affection. There wasn't any specific turning point, but we believe years of a safe environment with positive reinforcement built her confidence to trust these selected human beings. She also developed trust for members of her pack, which had proven not to be a threat. Her pack mates were there every day and became a source of support.

As she developed greater confidence, her behavior toward our vacuum cleaner changed, too. After two years of living in our house, she finally stopped attacking the vacuum cleaner. She would simply leave the room which was being vacuumed and find a more isolated area of the house. Several years later, she would lie on the floor and just simply watch the device as it was pushed around the room. After years of being kept safe and not being teased, she had become confident the vacuum was not a threat. This may seem like a small accomplishment, but it is significant progress for such a scared dog.

After two years, she began to allow us to touch her.

After three years, she sought out physical attention.

After four years, she would attempt to crawl in our lap.

Despite all of the progress Mea has made, it is confined to our house or only when under the close supervision of strong leaders. When she has to deal with new experiences outside of strong leadership, she reverts to her former behavior. Mea can never be trusted not to attack a dog or human on first meeting. She will never possess the confidence to accept others without being scared and possibly lashing out.

Mea is an example of Bully Behavior.

At the writing of this book, Mea continued to be a member of our pack. Over the 8+ years she lived with us we have kept her in a safe predictable environment. Either old age or a feeling of safety has mellowed Mea's behavior. But she will never have confidence.

HAROLD

Harold's father was very autocratic, dictating orders and not listening for others opinions. He handed out orders and expectations to family members. The relationship between his parents was more like a boss and servant than equal partnership.

His father also had a very harsh temper, when things did not go his way, involving yelling and screaming. I am not sure if there was any physical abuse in the family but mental abuse certainly existed.

When Harold got in trouble at school his father would blame teachers and principals as it was there fault and not his son's At home, his father would go into a tirade on Harold for the shame and embarrassment he has caused his father.

As Junior High age kids we avoided going to Harold's house because none of us liked being around his father.

Like his father, Harold bragged a lot about everything. They both had an exaggerated perspective of their accomplishments. Neither accepted criticism, berating anyone who expressed an alternative opinion.

Those who have to brag about themselves have very little to talk about

At the same time Harold always had money. It seemed that his father used money as compensation for his abusive behavior. Or maybe the money was an attempt to impress Harold's friends.

Harold was never in need or want for anything, he always seemed to get the inanimate objects in life he needed, clothes, cars, etc. Harold learned to be tough and to survive. He kept others away, and never allowed himself to get close to anyone. On initial meeting, he would snap out in an aggressive manner to scare the new acquaintance. Harold was the prototypical bully. He liked showing off how macho he was by talking down to others, or by making threating and insulting comments. It was common for him to point at others and laugh while making rude comments.

Early in life, he observed those who bullied, possibly his father to his mother, could intimidate other people and get their way. His first experience bullying another person took place when he was very young and it worked, Harold got his way, thus rewarding him for his behavior. By the time he was in elementary school, the aggressive pattern had been reinforced frequently enough to make it his standard behavior.

In junior high school, Harold was small in stature, neat in appearance, but bold in attitude. He was quick to make negative comments about others. He had developed a behavior of targeting those he felt were a threat or sensed were vulnerable. He would use mean names to describe other people's appearance or behavior, making those people feel uncomfortable. Calling other people derogatory names was a defense mechanism to scare others. He would use information against people.

Harold was a loner. He was always on the offensive, trying to pick fights with anyone and everyone. He liked threatening fights and fighting. Seldom did physical encounters actually take place, but threats of physical violence were constant. When physical violence did take place, it was via a sneak attack or with the backing of a mob. This behavior kept him socially immature. He was unable to carry on long conversations instead frequently resorting to sharp quips.

As a student he was average. He tried to raise himself up by putting others down. Saying cruel things about other people made him feel good about himself. Being cruel to others provided a better feeling than if he was to receive praise or recognition for an accomplishment. Harold had very low self-esteem, and covered it by intimidating others with his aggressive side. Too often, this is perceived as confidence, it is not, it is just the opposite. The aggressive behavior is used in an attempt to cover paranoid fear.

Bullies are socially challenged

Several years after graduating from high school, Harold married an on-again-off-again girl friend from high school. The

215

How to Treat Your Employees Like a Dog

marriage lasted just a few years before he became abusive, more mentally than physically, while always trying to intimidate his wife. The marriage ultimately ended in divorce, and even after the divorce Harold would stalk his ex-wife. He would call her with threats, always trying to intimidate. He married a second time, which also resulted in an angry divorce. Because he lacked social skills, his relationships were based on appearance, the more attractive the more interested he became.

**What you have done in the past
is how you will act in the future.**

The same pattern continued with his jobs. He moved from employer to employer. Some time in his 30's he found employment with a manager who took a liking to Harold. Over the course of several years he ascended to a supervisory position. In this situation he surrounded himself with people who would not challenge his authority. Harold would frequently bring subordinates into his office to berate their work performance. Harold's interaction with others was finding fault in their work and making sure they were informed of such flaws. He was always looking for negative things to say about others. As in earlier times of his life, Harold would berate others by calling them names to embarrass or create negative self-image. Because Harold had low self-esteem he was very easily threatened by anyone displaying competence. So, he would only employ those who could easily be intimated and would not challenge any decision he made.

The behavior of finding fault in others and announcing those faults to as many others as possible is the common behavior of insecure scared people.

With peers as well as subordinates, one of his typical bullying tactics was to attack with a verbal barrage of insults then to disappear, leaving those who were the victim of such attacks left felling vulnerable and embarrassed. Out of nowhere, Harold would erupt into a screaming episode focusing his anger on a subordinate. He would yell and scream like a 4 year old having a temper tantrum. Such behavior by an adult is completely shocking and leaves observers stunned. As quickly as he would appear with a red-faced eruption of childish behavior, he would then just as quickly retreat and disappear to his office.

Fear does not produce respect, it produces distrust.

After being a recipient of such attacks, most people did not pursue the departing raging Harold, they were simply happy Harold left the scene. This childish behavior caused distrust of those around him. Turnover in his department was common and those who continued to work for him did so in a cautious manner. His department only produced new ideas if they were Harold's. Subordinates learned not to show initiative or risk being victims of a temper tantrum.

Harold tried to keep his staff from knowing anything was taking place in the company. If Harold was the only one with access to information he could make himself appear more important than he really was. In addition, he would constantly provide misinformation to staff to create distrust between employees and confusion. This included such simple things as his calendar, which was also kept a secret. If he had to travel to attend meetings he would not share his arrive or departure schedule. This type of behavior is referred to as Mushroom Management, keeping staff in the dark and feeding the, manure.

Harold immediately took credit for any ideas coming from his department which received any positive recognition. The same was true of his ability to plagiarize the work of others. Harold was quick to take credit for any accomplishment regardless of who was the author. He would even take credit for accomplishments from other departments outside of his responsibility. Due to his plagiarism, his staff kept any new ideas to themselves.

The opposite was also the case. When a project or idea from Harold's department was proven to be a failure he was quick to blame others. He made sure everyone knew he never made mistakes. Any errors were the result of people in his department not properly keeping him informed.

Bullies lie often and without remorse.

As tempting as it was to bully him back, or retaliate with name calling or temper tantrums, few people ever did. Due to fear, most people tried to make Harold feel more respected than he actually was, such as pretending to listen to his opinions, but they were always on guard not to trust him. Those who had to work in the same department tried to avoid working close to him. The gossip regarding Harold and how to avoid working anywhere near him was daily activity by many of the organization members. This behavior galvanized most of the company employees to develop an us-versus-Harold behavior. The informal organization was galvanized, constantly communicating ways to work around Harold rather than work with him.

His behavior drove away talented staff in his department. The only people who worked for him long term, were scared drones agreeing with everything Harold proposed. Over time, Harold's department became an example of mediocracy.

Intimidation was his best skill. But when people did not back down to the bullying tactics he was quick to back off. Fear was the basis for his behavior. People who are aggressive are so because they are scared.

These are not the characteristics of leadership, yet I am amazed at the number of Harold's I have met in leadership positions whose bullying behavior destroys the company where they worked.

Bullies are very prevalent in our society and for some reason people mistake such behavior as strength.

Bully behavior is a display of cowardice and fear.

Harold perpetually boasted to his boss's he was the company's most valuable asset. A common behavior Harold repeated was that after he had establish tenure with a company, Harold threatened, his bosses, to quit if his compensation wasn't improved, insisting the company would suffer without him. Most of these threats were answered with the compensation he requested. But a couple times his bosses refused, forcing Harold to depart. In such cases the bosses initial concern, what if Harold's claims might be correct; his departure would inflict a decline in business. In those situations, upon Harold's departure, company morale, production, and revenue improved. With the departure of Harold, the rest of the employees became more productive. After Harold's departure, everyone began working as a team more cooperatively, the business's as a whole flourished. Employee's comments were "it was about time".

It was about time!

He had never received positive reinforcement for acting courteous, so he was unable to reward or thank others. Acting as a bully is a behavior used to keep others from seeing how scared and insecure he really was. But in reality, Harold a very fearful individual.

Bullies

Mea and Harold are very similar. Both were born as lower members of their pack, probably Omegas. This is important to keep in mind when looking at how bully behavior is developed. Both grew up

219

feeling they either had no one to protect them or rely on for help. Both developed an attitude of attacking first as the most effective means of self-protection. They learned early in life not expose themselves to anyone. They both believed if others feared them, then they had power.

Entitlement

Bullies are a result of their young environment. A child under the age of seven who repeatedly observes abusive behavior by adults is likely to learn from the behavior they see and repeat such behavior. When a young child is allowed to mimic such behavior without receiving corrections, they will then internalize such behavior. Weeks of repeating such behavior without reprimand will produce bullying tendencies. If allowed to continue over extended lengths of time through their development period, they have a very strong chance of carrying these tendencies throughout the rest of their lives. Bullies often are a result of children who were not taught proper interpersonal skills or were never corrected when behaving inappropriately.

Entitlement is also a cause for bulling behavior. Entitlement is actually a form of mental abuse. Children who are raised in an entitlement environment; where they are not held responsible for their actions; never develop a moral compass. These are children who lack the ethical role models who will take responsibility for teaching social conduct by their behavior and hold the child accountable for their behavior.

Entitlement has a potential to produce bully behavior.

Think of the 2-year-old child throwing a temper tantrum. How the child's parents or nearby adults react toward this behavior will impact future behavior. If Mom panics and provides the child with attention, she has just rewarded the child for having a temper tantrum and has taught the child throwing a temper tantrum gets attention and rewards. After a month of such behavior, which is followed by rewards, the temper tantrum has become a habit, and will continue to be used through life.

In contrast, when a puppy displays undesirable behavior, the closest adult dog will correct the behavior by picking up the problem puppy by the nape of the neck and giving it a firm shake. This is to let the puppy know such behavior is not acceptable. The problem is solved and everyone moves on. In the wild, a dog pack needs to work as a team and understands all members of the pack need to display the appropriate behavior if they are to survive.

Bullies do not accept responsibility for their actions.

In too many cases, bullies are able to intimidate peers to the point of receiving a formal management title. Titles are very important for bullies believing it makes them superior to others. When given a formal title, bullies will prey on others in subordinate positions. Studies indicate 75 percent of work place bullying is done by someone in a supervisory role. If bullies are allowed to function without strong supervision, their behavior to posture over others will occur.

Bullying behavior can be controlled if there is strong supervision. Micromanaging and constantly monitoring the bully's behavior as well as listening closely to the bully's subordinates, can help. Bullies do not respect others, regardless of the other person's experience or knowledge. Bullies who fear their supervisor or a person who has the authority to fire them, are less likely to display the bullying traits in the workplace, but will instead display their bully behavior in other settings, such as at home. A strong parental-supervisory figure can keep the bullies from displaying intimidation traits on others. The problem, bullies cannot control themselves, even with strong supervision they will still have break through episodes in which they erupt with bullying behavior toward subordinates.

221

Bullies blame others for their mistakes.

Bulling behavior is indicative of those who are scared and very insecure; they are always on the offensive in an effort to intimidate others. After years of attacking first to make themselves feel safer, this behavior becomes self-rewarding. This repeated behavior builds a life-long habit.

Another characteristic of bullies is in their own minds they are never wrong. They frequently lie to protect the belief they are always right. Bullies confidently tell different lies to different people and lash out and attack if such lies are challenged. When they are wrong and make mistakes, they are very quick to point blame toward others. Bullies are quick to identify the weakest people around them and direct blame for any wrongs on their weaker peers and subordinates. When held accountable, bullies will redirect conversation to point blame at other person or use someone else as a scape goat. They are very quick to find fault in others, thus, constantly keeping everyone else around them on the defensive.

Bullies lie often.

Bullies have a tendency to erupt into temper tantrums, at any time, for any reason. Their behavior is very inconsistent. Bullies involvement in an organization creates a very distrustful environment. Those who work in organizations in which bullies are allowed to exist become defensive, constantly working with caution. Working in an organization allowing bullies to exist, will never develop employees who will work to their fullest potential. Organizations with bullies will struggle with morale and generally experience high employee turnover.

Resource guarding

Resource guarding is a behavior which scared people and dogs exhibit. They will become aggressive to others who try to encroach on their possessions. In humans this is displayed by a bully trying to keep his boss from talking with other company employees – especially his subordinates. Because bullies frequently lie, it is safest if the people they have lied to, never talk with each other.

The resource guarded by dogs is most often involves food or toys, but it can also be someone's attention. With humans, the most often guarded resource is information or access to someone of importance. If they can control information and keep it from co-workers they feel a sense of power to use over others.

Targeting

Targeting is when bullies focusing their attention on another individual they feel poses a threat or one who is weak and vulnerable. In dogs, they will stare at the targeted subject in an erect posture acting agitated. Dogs in the process of targeting usually have raised hair on the back of their neck and may expose teeth or drool. If not restrained, they will charge and attack. When targeting, humans follow a similar pattern focusing attention on the targeted individual and displaying an aggressive posture. Humans use verbal barbs or rude comments to attack the targeted subject.

Mushroom Management

This is a management style of weak and scared managers who attempt to amass power by keeping subordinates in the dark. Bullies do not share information with others. At the same time they create rumors and lies to cause confusion. Thus, the practice of keeping people in the dark and feeding them manure, the environment where mushrooms flourish, has become the term Mushroom management.

What took so long?

Bullies also exaggerate their importance. They like to brag about their title or the importance of their job. Bullies spend a lot of time guarding access of communication to people in positions above themselves on the organization chart. Bullies always present themselves to their superiors as being the company's most important employee creating the impression if they were to leave, the company will suffer. In most cases, the bully has convinced the business owner or president he or she is irreplaceable.

Companies with leadership who are so convinced of these claims will make special compensations, providing special perks, pay raise, etc. when the bully threatens to leave the company. On those occasions where the leadership gets tired of such threats or does not succumb to the bully's extortion and they terminate the bully, the response by the rest of the organization is what took so long? Then what usually happens is the remaining staff, as a group, increases productive behavior.

So when the bully is finally terminated, the informal organization responds in a positive way.

Behavior begets behavior

Bullies are a result of their early environment. The longer they are allowed to bully, or worse, are encouraged to bully, the deeper entrenched the behavior becomes. If the pattern is allowed to continue after age seven, a bully will be a bully for life. If under the supervision of a strong respected leader their bulling behavior may be controlled. But if a control figure is not diligent, or if removed, the bully will revert to bully behavior.

A person's value system is established early in life. The first seven years of life are very important to how a person will act the rest of their life. So, how a 7 year old behaves is going to be very similar to how that same person will act when they are 70 years old. The only thing changing is the effect their behavior can have on others. The behavior they project and attributes they most internalize as important are securely in place. Like an amplifier, the more power or money a person possesses the stronger these values are displayed.

Money/power makes people more of what they are.
Those who are philanthropic will give more.
Those who are bullies will attack more.
Those who have a drug problem will become addicted.
Those with a drinking problem will become an alcoholic.
Those who volunteer their time will give more of themselves.

So when a bully obtains power or wealth their behavior becomes even more exaggerated. The example of people who amass great wealth in a short period of time, they have more money to spend on favorite activities. If they enjoyed gambling, the bets and losses become greater. If it is drug use, the amount is greater.

In contrast, those who give of themselves and experience great wealth become even more philanthropic, helping those less fortunate than themselves. Examples are Bill Gates or Warren Buffet who contribute huge amounts of money to charitable causes.

Bullies are very scared.
Bullies are insecure.
Bullies live in fear.
Bullies are a result of entitlement
Bullies are a result of abuse.
Bullies make terrible leaders.

When put in a position of leadership, bullies will destroy an organization.

Communicate in the language of the listener

Chapter Eleven

PAULA

We were contacted regarding a puppy mill that had been shut down and the dogs from the breeding farm would need homes. The next day we received a female golden retriever who had spent her entire life as a breeding bitch in an outdoors fenced in pen. She was a very cute, puppy faced, smallish frame Golden Retriever. Based on her appearance she was probably two or three years old.

Her life had been spent penned up in an outdoor fenced in area with other dogs, which means she probably was bred every time she came into season. From the feces imbedded in her coat, ears and paws the pen probably had never been cleaned. The smell of feces reeked off her. So the first order of business was to at least make her more pleasant to be near. We would not bring her into our house until we could get control of the odor. This was years of embedded feces and the smell was not going away easy.

Her first day with us was spent clipping out matted coat which was embedded with feces and mud, followed by lathering, rinsing, and more trimming and then repeat the bathing procedure. The totally petrified scared dog who had never had this much human contact, patiently tolerated our every request. She probably had never been bathed, yet as scary as it had to be for her, she continued to fully cooperate. After a full day of grooming and cleaning, she still smelled, maybe a little better, but still really bad, so we kenneled her in the garage. For another day we bathed and trimmed her coat trying to get the imbedded feces and odor. Based on her physical appearance she had several litters of puppies. Throughout this whole process she was very fearful of humans but never retaliated or fought our attempts to help her.

After three days of work, she smelled pleasant enough so we could bring her into our house. Because she had not been house broken nor did she have any house experience we kept her confined to our tile floor laundry room. In addition, she feared the presents of humans, so whenever a human would enter the laundry room she would crawl on her belly and submissively urinate.

The new foster still did not have a name; we just weren't able to come up with a fitting name, so we just referred to her as the new dog. Bonnie's father, Paul, was the person who introduced Bonnie to dogs and dog training. Bonnie's first step-mother came with a well-trained Doberman Pincher; Mindy which is what set the stage for Bonnie's future dog expectations. Paul was the person who picked out Bonnie's first dog, a Golden Retriever named Rebel, who she trained in obedience at 4-H club. By now you are probably beginning to get the idea; Paul was a dog lover, always interested in the new members of our pack. At this point in life, Paul was in his 90's, living in assisted living, but still curious about Bonnie's newest canine challenge. When explaining to Paul the newest project, a smallish, golden retriever puppy mill refugee he took special interest wanting to help. It is for this reason the new puppy was named Paula. Paula became a frequent topic of conversation with Paul showing pictures and updating him on her progress.

It took several weeks of Paula spending her life in our laundry room with short visits from the other members of our dog pack to integrate her into indoor pet life. Since she had spent her life is a small confined area, she did not try to escape or break out of the laundry room. Paula continued to fear humans as they neared her by crawling on her belly and submissively urinating. Over time she appeared to have gained confidence because she felt safe and her environment was consistent.

Rehabilitating her to become a pet was looking like a long term project. Paula was very sweet and never showed any signs of aggressive behavior, but how long will it take for her to become comfortable with human. We did not want to subject her to a lot of stress with constant attention, but we did want her gain the confidence to tolerate the presents of humans.

After two months, not much had changed in her reaction to humans. Her appearance was getting much better, especially since in the initial cleaning process we had cut out chunks of her dry brittle coat, to remove mats and feces which were now growing back fuller. Paula was now on a better diet and exercise routine her coat was growing in shinier and fuller.

Somewhere in the third month Paula's confidence began to show, as she would wag her tail and not cower when a human would enter her laundry room. She had also become much more confident with the other members of her pack. Occasionally she would even walk toward the entering human hoping to receive some petting attention. Shortly after this breakthrough it was time to start introducing new humans into her life. We had a neighbor family, of four, which included a five year old daughter and seven year old son, they frequently expressed interest in the fosters which came and went through our house. We thought they would make good test subjects for Paula to meet. The initial meeting went well. Such visits continued whenever possible.

You have probably already figured out what happened next, the neighbors adopted Paula and took her home on Christmas Eve. They had the option to change her name but kept the name Paula, because by now she had become a Paula.

After the adoption, in her new pack, Paula's confidence soared. Paula became a frequent spectator at their kid's soccer, little league baseball games as well as many other family events. Based on the number of comments from neighbors telling how they meet Paula, she had become a local celebrity due to the number of community activities she attended with her family. To the point we were receiving frequent requests from people who met Paula asking how they could get a Paula. Special dogs like Paula are not easy to find.

Several years after the adoption Paula's family had to go out of town for a few days and asked if Paula could stay with us while they were gone. This was an easy yes. On the second day of her sleep over, at our house, we had a visit from one of our dog show friends. She showed up with two young puppies she wanted us to see. They were adorable.

At this time our pack consisted of four adult female Golden Retrievers, plus visiting Paula and these two puppies in our house. After initial greetings the humans became engrossed in conversation and stopped paying close attention to the every move of the cute puppies. Being puppies they began to misbehave, nipping and biting, our four female adult dogs were spayed and none of them had ever been bred. The four observed the misbehaving puppies not knowing how to react they stood petrified by this experience. It did not take much time for Paula to take charge, she quickly, directly, in a motherly way corrected the puppy's behavior. Paula's communication with the puppies was clear and fully understood. The puppies recognized Paula's instructions and responded with respect to her expectations. They quickly received the message such behavior was not to be tolerated. At the same time our four adult female dogs looked on as spectators from a distance in awe. They looked at each other as if to say, how did she do that.

Actions speaks louder than words

Paula had the experience of being a mother. As a puppy mill bitch she had multiple litters. In these situations she was totally responsible for the care and feeding of her puppies and understood how to handle any misbehavior. This was not a new experience to her. She understood puppy behavior and how to communicate with them. Paula communicated directly as to what behavior was acceptable and what was not. The puppies totally understood Paula's expectations and followed her directions. Paula was confident and clear with her communication. She knew what she was doing and she understood how to communicate. For the remainder of the time the puppies and Paula were together in our house everything was quiet and under control.

The most important ingredient in the formula of success is knowing how to get along with others.
Theodore Roosevelt.

The remainder of her sleep over was uneventful. But she proved to be an excellent doggie baby sitter. When her family returned home she went back to her now normal life as a family member.

After being adopted from our foster care, Paula enjoyed the good life. She had become an integral member the adopting family, so much so, after ten years with her new pack, when the son of her adopted family graduated from high school, Paula was included in his graduation pictures. In all, Paula lived with her adopted family nearly twelve years, to a ripe old age of at best guess about fifteen years old.

Through those years she had brought a lot of happiness too many people.

PILOT

It was a typical Friday evening at the airport, after a week of business travel I was boarding a flight home. I was tired and anxious to get home. By the appearance of the passengers around me, they felt the same as I, it had been a long work week and we wanted to get home. My feeling regarding Friday evening flights, after a week away from home, is similar to the majority of people; we just want to get home. From the start all went according to plan, we boarded, taxied, and took-off, on schedule, excellent.

About the time I usually expect to feel the aircraft begin to change altitude in preparation for landing it just did not seem typical. It seemed like this flight was making a few more changes in direction than normal, then the pilot made an intercom announcement "you may have noticed we are circling over Nebraska, because a storm has closed Denver's airport". He continued to keep the passenger informed with flight progress (or lack thereof) announcements about every five to ten minutes. He continued to provide updates as to the changing weather in Denver and airport situation.

The feeling of knowing what is happening seemed to reduce some of the passengers complaining. Though we did not have control of our situation we at least felt involved. Then we received the announcement the aircrafts fuel was getting low and we needed to land soon. Since Denver was not an option, the pilot announced his plan to land and refuel in Colorado Springs, which was unaffected by the severe weather. He negotiated a landing time with the air traffic controller, all the while giving us frequent updates. Just prior to the landing approached he continued to keep us informed as to what we should expect after landing.

There were other flights which had also been diverted from Denver to Colorado Springs, which we could see on approach. After landing and taxiing to a parking location the pilot announced he was leaving the aircraft to negotiate for fuel. He explained the galley would offer free drinks and treats while he was away from the aircraft. He was very serious in his explanation; stating after we were refueled the time scheduled by air traffic controllers for departure may not provide a lot of time for preparation. The pilot went on to explain, when I say we need everyone in their seats and ready to depart you need to respond immediately.

Through the entire process this pilot kept his crew and passengers fully informed and involved in the events impacting our lives. The pilot knew what to do; he gave instructions to the co-pilot, flight attendance as well as the passengers. He was great.

As he passed through the entire cabin departed out stairs at the rear of the plane for fuel, the passengers in the cabin acted like teenagers at a pep rally. We were cheering our pilot, applauding and chanting GO! GO! GO! The pilot passed through the cabin like a hero.

It was hard to grasp, these are people, who all had plans for their Friday night, expecting to go home, which had been totally derailed. They were already late getting home, stuck in a metal tube, on the tarmac at Colorado Springs Airport instead of at home with family and or friends. Yet, they were cheering their hero on like a running back heading for the end zone and not complaining about their situation. We all could have something to complain about, but instead the unplanned landing turned into one of the oddest happy hours of my life. Why was this behavior so civil and cooperative? The pilot's communication, kept us feeling involved and not wondering what is going on, was the difference.

Lack of communication creates rumors and anxiety

When the pilot returned to the flight, he entered up the rear stairs, then using the aircrafts rear microphone he explained the actions he had taken with the ground crew. He was going to exit the plane again to insure everything was proceeding as expected.

While the pilot was outside of the aircraft some of the passengers, sitting in widow seats, were updating the rest of us as to what was taking place. We were getting a play by play description of our pilot and ground crews progress. The window announcers alerted the rest of us our pilot was making his second return back on the plane.

As he walked through the crowded cabin it was like Moses parting the red sea, everyone moved out of the aisle so as not to impede his progress. While walking through the aisle he was greeted with smiling passengers, high fives, pats on the back, cheering and accolades.

Before returning to the cockpit he turned stood at the front of the cabin in front of the passengers waved his hands to be quiet, which we responded to immediately. Then, without a microphone, he announced to the entire plane some more paper work had to be completed and communication with air traffic controllers had to be conducted, but when he was given a departure time everyone must get into their seat ready for takeoff.

Just as instructed earlier; when he gave the word, telling passenger they needed to prepare for take-off, everyone acted exactly as told. During the process passengers were polite picking up any dropped napkins, straws, cups, helping flight crew as much as possible to be neat. The pilot had given us a sense of responsibility and we did not want to disappoint him.

When trust is high communication is easy

During this unplanned lay over and after hours cocktail party, I believe there were several business deals made between newly found customers and clients who were introduced to each other while waiting to be refueled. There were many new friends made and the exchange of some great jokes; it turned out to be a fun experience.

Why should such an unplanned inconvenience turn out so pleasant? It was due to the pilot, who took charge of the situation treating his passengers with the respect; keeping all informed and involved. Our pilot demonstrated leadership, taking responsibility, and understanding the inconvenience everyone on the plane had experienced he reduced tension by using purposeful communications.

Communications

In my many travel experiences when unexpected surprise occur the pilot usually hides in the cockpit and shares nothing, which causes passengers to think the worst, leading to worry and complaints. Unexpected events happen in everyone's life. Complaints by customers usually revolve more around how the company responded to the event, often feeling disrespected by not having a sense of involvement, than they do about the actual event causing the inconvenience.

The best surprise is no surprise.

A 2017 Gallup survey of the US workplace found 67% US managers who say they don't like talking with employees, which mirrors the 67% of US workers who say they're not engaged at work. That figure comes from the most recent, annual in-depth report of more than 31 million workers across US industries.

Only 13% of respondents in the Gallup survey said that their company's leadership communicates effectively with the rest of the organization. Those employees who did report having conversations with their manager in the previous six months about their goals and successes were 2.8 times more likely to be engaged at work.

"Organizations are realizing that more frequent, ongoing conversations may be the missing link in performance management, but there is a huge caveat: Managers have to understand *how* to have effective performance conversations with employees," the report read. "Unfortunately, Gallup research suggests that many managers struggle in this area."

37% of business time is spent correcting mistakes.

W. Edward Deming

Engineer/Author

Painful as the interactions may be for managers, Gallup's research found that employees do, in fact, want to have conversations with the people they report to at work. The organization suggests manager's check in with employees individually at least once a week. Workers want relevant feedback on their performance, clear discussion of goals, and the freedom to approach their manager with questions.

60% of business failures are due to poor communications.

Peter Drucker

In today's environment we have a wider array of options as medium for communications, but the variety of options does not improve delivery of the message. Just because we have greater variety of methods to deliver a message is not a guarantee the message will be correctly received. Companies have found baby boomers are better at delivering face to face message than millennials. The same is true for the message details. Millennials have learned to communicate using abbreviations which are easily misunderstood. They also prefer to use electronic medium. Successful communications needs to be done in a simple universally understood terms, yet detailed enough to have just one meaning.

Successful Communications

Simplify-Simplify-Simplify

Successful communication needs to be simplified. Keep the message simple to understand. By keeping it simple helps to insure the message has one meaning. The message cannot be interpreted in a variety of ways by the recipient. Paula delivered her message to the puppies in a very simple and clear.

Frequency

If the message is important it needs to be sent to the recipient on a regular basis. Numerous reminders of the message can be done utilizing a variety of communication mediums. As our pilot reinforced his expectation of the passengers, delivery of an easy to understand message needs done with a frequency which best fits the purpose of message and the audience.

Consistency

When a leader creates a message it is important to have consistency among staff linking pins to insure they are delivering the message as it was intended. As demonstrated by the game telephone, when a message is passed from one individual to another the initial message becomes distorted. Each person the message passes through, unintentionally, interjects person prejudices, which slightly alters the original meaning. When sending a message which has the potential to get passed through multiple people it is important to insure each person given the responsibility to continue transmitting the message does so correctly, not distorting the message.

Honesty

Keep your promises and be consistent if you want to be trusted. If the speaker has the trust of the audience both the attention

237

to the message and commitment to the message will be much improved over someone who does not have the trust of the audience. Speakers with a reputation of honesty are more successful at delivering an accurately received message.

Listen to the Audience

After a message has been sent, it is important to read the reaction of the audience. Is there a vehicle to receive feedback from the audience to insure they received the intended message? Did the audience correctly understand the message? Was the audience given the opportunity to respond to the message and ask questions? In small groups this is easier than large audiences. Small groups can simply be asked for immediate feedback. Larger groups require much more formal means of data collection, such as survey's, questioners or smaller breakout groups.

Non-Verbal Communications (Neurolinguistics)

An important component, when possible, to an effective delivery of a message involves the non-verbal message. Paula's message was primarily non-verbal, direct and well understood by the puppies, and a learning experience for the other four adult female dogs.

In the case of our pilot, his non-verbal communication made his message so much more effective. He stood outside of the cockpit, in front of the passengers, delivering his plan of action including instructions to crew and passengers. Then he departed the aircraft to speak directly with the ground crew to negotiate for needed services. He could have stayed in the cockpit when speaking to those on the aircraft. He also could have stayed in the cockpit and speak to ground crew personnel to receive the needed services. None of us on the aircraft will ever know if leaving the plane to speak face to face with the ground crew made any difference in the promptness of the services we received, but it gave the impression he cared and wanted to get all of us to our destination. The non-verbal actions exhibited by our pilot projected an image of leadership. His confidence and take charge attitude produced commitment from everyone on the plane to support his plan. People like to help people they trust.

10% of conflicts are due to a difference of opinion; 90% is due to tone of voice and delivery.

Communication is improved when the audience trusts and respects the presenter. When the audience can see the speaker there is a much better chance to develop such trust. In an earlier chapter, Julie, I pointed out how speech needs to be slower when the speaker cannot be seen, compared to when the speaker is visible.

A speaker posture influences the audience's perception of the message, as to the seriousness and trustworthiness. Posture is also important for listeners. Straight posture either sitting or standing while listening improves retention of the message being received. This is even true when communicating on a phone. Observe someone speaking on the phone to an important customer or persons boss, they are most often sitting up straight or standing erect. When conversing on the phone with a casual acquaintance the posture of each is most often very relaxed, possibly slouched, leaning against a wall or leaning back in a chair.

Facial expressions and hand gestures play a very valuable role in perception of the message. Hand gestures are used to underscore or emphasize a message. When a speaker palms are exposed while delivering a message the received message is more believable. Speakers who hide the palms of their hands while speaking is interpreted message are received as distrustful.

Open communication involves open palm but also include uncrossed arms and legs. People who speak with both arms and legs

239

uncrossed are most likely honest. Listeners with uncrossed arms and legs are most open to active listening.

When a communicator speaks with crossed arms they are not fully honest and are covering up something. The same occurs with crossed legs; the speaker is protecting information and is guarded at what they will say. Listeners with a similar closed posture are not listening but building defenses from hearing what is being said. When both arms and legs are tightly crossed this is called cocooning. People who assume a cocooning posture while speaking, are lying or telling as little of the truth as possible. Those cocooning as a listener are extremely defensive, not wanting to believe the speaker position.

Smiles with wide eyes draw people closer and lighten the message. Compared to when a speaker frowns with squinted eyes, most people will back away and receive the message with caution. People who stare are also perceived as aggressive and hostile which also impedes open communication.

Most important to delivering and receiving a face to face message is the positioning of each person's hips. Where the hips face the brain follows. Information retention is improved when the listener squares their hip to the speaker. This is true of small group conversation or in a lecture hall. Large meeting room audience's members who square their hips with the speaker, knees bent and square with an erect posture leaning slightly forward typically retain more of the message being delivered by the orator than of someone whose hip are not square to the speaker and posture is slouching or leaning backward.

Mis-Communications (polluted message)

When communication is incomplete of important information or it the message is not organized in an easy to understand format mis-communication occurs. Common problems with mis-communication in a message:

Missing information:

It is very easy to omit important information in a communication message when it is at the end of a thought. Information which is familiar or is taken for granted that the sender assumes the receiver should automatically know is easily omitted. For example when dates are a function of the message, the year can be forgotten. Same is true of a communication which includes a location cities can be given without a state. When in a hurry it is easy to forget to include such data.

Incorrect information:

This can occur when as a linking pin member of a communication chain does not accurately relay information. Information is received and then passed on to another person or group either in verbal or written form which was flawed to start, then perpetuates the incorrect information. When receiving information it is important to insure what has been received is correct. It also occurs in the transfer of information if the intermediate member unconsciously alters the information transmitted.

Mis-spelled word especially people's names:

It is flattering to hear ones name being spoken. It is also very insulting when others mis-spell or incorrectly pronounces a person's name. Receiving a message beginning with a mis-pronounced or mis-spelled name the receiver immediately is distracted from clearly listening to what follows. Even more important, messages which begin with a wrongly pronounced or spelled name, the receiver begins to distrust whatever follows. This usually occurs when the communicator is in a hurry or does not do their research. An example is when I receive written communication intended for my wife Mrs. Hornfisher but it is addressed Mr. Hornfisher. All it takes in missing one letter to create a lot of confusion.

Clutter information:

More talk does not constitute better communication. Words can be a source of misunderstanding. This includes information not relevant to the purpose of the communication. The difference between communicating with the correct words versus the almost correct words is the difference between lightening and a lightening bug.

Slang and acronyms:

There is a difference between simplifying communication and shortening a message. Slang and acronyms can be interpreted different ways based on a person past experience. Googling an acronym or slang term usually produces a variety of responses. In previous chapters of this book I have used words such as bitch and intact. To people who a not familiar with the dog world, these words, could be offended or confused by such words.

Assumptions:

Face to face communication reduces the incidence of assumption occurring because the message sender can visually assess how the message is being received. When the receiver looks confused the sender can inquire as to the problem. This is why it is important to collect feedback on sent messages to confirm the message was received as it was intended by the sender.

Constant talk is not communication

Information Overload

With the ever increasing modes and availability of communications we are entangled in information overload. How much of the constant barrage of information being presented to us is really important. Most of us have daily access to hundreds of television stations on air 24/7 competing for our viewership. Radio stations are equally similar. There are an ever growing number of social media options. What is need to know information versus nice to know information. Most of the benefits social media presents to us are nice to know information which is primarily entertainment.

Creating Commitment

Like delivering a formal presentation; when sharing a plan with others, whose involvement is required for success of the project, the method of communication needs to be done both verbally and written. It is also helpful to tell people what you are going to tell them, tell them, then, tell them what you just told them. It sound very redundant but repeating similar information reduces misunderstandings. Our pilot understood repeated the same message multiple times but in different ways to insure everyone was properly informed.

Getting the best players is easy; getting them to work together is tough.

Casey Stengel

Leaders of all size organizations agree, creating a plan of action is easy; the challenge is getting those responsible for executing the plans to buy in and committing themselves. Good leaders identify problems and design appropriate responses to solve those problems. But it is the great leaders who can then stimulate a commitment by those who have to put the plan into practice. Getting unity of staff in the implementation of a program is very difficult. The four most common obstacles to successful communication of a plan include

1) People don't totally understand what they are supposed to do. They misunderstand the directives which are pertaining to their specific involvement. If communication is not delivered in a forum which is easy to understand employees with distort the expectations. The environment it is delivered also affects the perceived benefits to drawbacks.

2) The people expected to participate in the program do not receive the proper training to conduct the program. They do not feel confidence in their personal skills to change their behavior as requested by the new program so they revert to former work behavior. If not properly trained they might only employ part of the skills needed to implement the new program.

3) If there are unexpected obstacles to the new program employees will resist commitment to the new program. When a new program is introduced the communicator needs prepare staff for obstacles and keep them informed how to respond. This is where proofing is used to prepare for the unexpected.

4) If the communicator does not present a convincing reason for the new program and stimulate buy in from informal leaders the majority of employee's response will be negative. People do not like change, so initial natural response by most is, I don't want to. This is where the communicator needs to assess his/her audience and utilize informal leader's participation early on in the planning process and use their support to help avoid negative response from the larger staff.

Creating solutions is easy; getting cooperation to execute the plan is difficult

Communication with subordinates should be honest and immediate. When recognition for desired behavior is deserved reward should be given. When feedback for undesired behavior is needed that too should be done immediately and specific. Waiting extended periods of time to provide feedback does not enhance performance. A problem many organizations have is saving feedback till and annual review, by then the opportunity for improvement has been lost. As

Paula illustrated, she was direct and timely with her feedback to the puppies. The puppies received the correction and responded appropriately. By their response she had their respect.

A player should never be surprised when they get cut.

Don Shula

Each of us is the only person who can solve our own problems.

Chapter Twelve

BECKY

While watching an outdoor agility match, Bonnie and I became involved in a conversation with two friends regarding a Nova Scotia Duck Tolling Retriever, (NSDTR or Toller), in need of a home. The two friends were Toller owners and one was a NSDTR breeder. The dog was currently kenneled at a local Humane Society.

The breeder had been contacted by the Humane Society to confirm the dog was really a NSDTR and it had been at their facility for several weeks. Today, there are DNA tests to determine what breed a dog is, but back at the time of this conversation took place such tests did not exist.

I am sure you see what's coming. The next day Bonnie went to visit the Toller at the Humane Society. On the door of the dog's crate was a big sign in red ink read: **I AM GOING BLIND.** This diagnosis was based on many tests which had been conducted on the dog. Many of the tests involved eye drops and other items placed in and around her eyes. They believed she had retinal degenerative disease. This is not a good diagnosis as there is no treatment to reverse it.

The Toller was about 18 months old and had been turned in by her owners because, she was going blind. Bonnie found the dog to be scared and a bit reactive to anyone getting close to her crate. This was not surprising, as most kennels are very stressful places with dogs barking and lunging at each other combined with a wide variety of humans doing all kinds of weird things.

This was a kill shelter (which mean due to the limited number of dog kennels and large number of dog admitted to shelter, relative to the number adopted, dog had to be euthanized when proved to be unadoptable) and the Toller had already overstayed the usual time most dogs would stay before being euthanized. They had kept the dog beyond her usual time because she was considered a rare breed. The shelter was aware The American Kennel Club was actively considering recognizing the NSDTR breed. Humane Society staff was hoping to find a rescue group to take her.

Bonnie's visit lasted about 30 minutes, the whole time the Toller kept her distance. She was not trusting, why should she? She was virtually blind staying in a strange place, with loud barking dogs, some of them lunging at her cage. Then there was the constant flow of unfamiliar people coming and going all around her cage. Who knows what other frightening things she heard and smelled during her time at the humane society?

Her first owner had abandoned her after nine months. Then several months later her second owner dropped her off at the Humane Society.

Dogs have the olfactory ability to smell scents of human remains in burial sites decades after burial. They can detect the odor of decaying bones, teeth and other grave remnants long after they have been buried. Such sniffer dogs are used to inspect potential construction sites for historic burial locations. With such an acute sense of smell, dogs are capable of deciphering the odor of recently euthanized dogs. This was an activity frequently occurring at this shelter. Such an environment makes it a highly stressful environment for a dog to live for a weeks. After eight weeks of it, this Toller was distrustful of everyone and everything around her.

Even though Bonnie's first encounter with the Toller had been a rather cold one, the dog had captured Bonnie's heart. The next day we returned and adopted this scared, blind, NSDTR and we named her Becky. But, before we could take her home, she had to be spayed, which added even more confusion and discomfort to her life.

When we returned the next day to take her home, she was sore from the incision, feeling even more vulnerable than she had over the past eight weeks. It took some time for her to trust us enough, just to get her into our car so we could transport her home. Next was the challenge of meeting her new pack of three dogs. One at a time, the pack members were introduced to Becky outside on the driveway. After plenty of sniffing and checking each other out, we were ready to take the pack into the house.

Becky was nervous, smelling everything, checking out all parts of the house, trying to make a mental road map. While she curiously examined her new surroundings, the rest of the pack seemed to understand what she was doing. They observed, with interest, her investigations and allowed her the space she needed to try to make sense of these new surroundings. As with every new entry to the pack, a lot of posturing takes place between the members to determine where they each fit.

Zeke, by default, as the only male, was the alpha male. Julie was the reining alpha female, which was well understood by all in the pack, and it appeared to be the same for Becky. The pack member most affected was Liz. Would she continue as the Beta female or would Becky take her position? This was where the most tension existed, between these two.

The first breakthrough toward building trust came in the most unusual form, Fred, the cat. Fred was a black-and-white shorthair we adopted to be the store cat when we owned Pet Outfitters. He was a very confident cat. He introduced himself to us when Pet Outfitters sponsored a mobile adoption day at the store. Fred adopted us. He made it very obvious he wanted to stay at the store and become a permanent employee. Over the years of working at Pet Outfitters, Fred displayed a very intuitive skill to understand dogs. Before he would approach and introduce himself to a dog he sized up if it was friendly or not. When Fred sensed a dog he could not trust he simply disappeared. It is with this background we used Fred as a valuable evaluator of foster dogs coming into our house.

Even at Becky's first entry into the house, Fred did not display any fear of her. So, even though Becky showed aggressive behavior toward other dogs at the Humane Society, Fred's behavior told us she was more distressed than aggressive. Within days of Becky's arrival, we would find Fred lying next to Becky as she slept in a dog bed. Fred became the first member of our pack Becky would trust. She trusted him long before trusting the rest of us. Fred's behavior was the bridge toward building trust with the rest of our pack.

What things could we do to help Becky function with her blindness? Bonnie and I were constantly thinking of things we could do to make her life easier. It was also important to keep her safe, so we restricted her access to particular areas of the house from such things as stairs.

After Becky had been living with us for a short time, we began our search for a canine ophthalmologist to evaluate her condition. During the initial exam, the veterinary staff began a series of tests including such things as test strips placed under her eye lids, drops in her eyes, probing, looking, holding, touching, and before these activities went very far, Becky reverted to her defensive behavior. The staff's immediate reaction was to muzzle the aggressive dog.

Fortunately, the Canine Ophthalmologist understood what was happening and ceased all testing. He explained the dog has been traumatized many times before when her eyes had been prodded and probed. He told us we needed to take her home and forget about any more eye tests until she developed more trust in people.

We took her back home, and worked on building routines in her life so she could trust other humans. Her meals were fed at the same time every day, in the same location. We kept the area of access in the house the same. We kept the furniture arrangement the same so it was easier to navigate. The goal is to keep her feeling safe. However, she continued to be defensive and distrustful.

Dogs, like children, want routines, it makes them feel safe.

In addition to building trust in the humans in her life, Becky was also developing trust in her pack members. In particular, the tall red-headed Golden Retriever named Liz with whom she initially had some of the greatest conflict. This was due to their similar positions in the pack. But over time, Liz took on the role as big sister to Becky. Becky met the breed standard of NSDTR with a shoulder height of 18", weight of about 35 pounds, red coat with white spots on her paws and chest, so she picked up the nickname of Little Red. Liz was the taller red head, 24" at the withers and about 65 pounds, and we referred to her as Big Red. Liz had also earned the reputation in the pack as the enforcer, but with Becky, Liz had become more of a mentor. Becky and Liz seemed to stay close to each other. The two dogs played together, slept near each other, and developed a trust in each other.

One of the most amazing events in this relationship was the two learned to run together in our yard, Liz in the lead with Becky's shoulder pressed against Liz's hip. Becky had learned to use Liz as a seeing-eye dog. They would run full speed around the open space of our back yard. Becky, with impaired vision, had developed a huge amount of trust in Liz she had become the protective older sister. Liz assessed Becky's impairment and the two created solutions to compensate.

Pack members can be trusted to take care of each other.

Several more months passed as we tried to keep her daily life as constant as possible, building her trust before we took her back to the canine ophthalmologist for a second time. After her first visit, the staff had placed a warning label on the front of Becky's file "Reactive – Muzzle. Now on this second visit, the ophthalmology staff was prepared placing a muzzle on her. Becky was scared. Yet this visit went much better despite being muzzled as a precaution. The exam and test found her blindness was not due to retinal degeneration, rather Juvenal onset cataracts, which could be corrected with surgery.

A date for surgery was established and we were given pre-surgery protocol to prepare the patient. Becky had to receive daily eye drops, which she did not like. The eye drops were not painful, but they did sting and were uncomfortable -- just another reason for her to become suspicious of humans.

The surgery would take place at the ophthalmologist's office, which was a change in her routine. Becky would have to be caged, at the ophthalmologist office, a foreign location, with strangers all around, and we worried about the potential of flash backs to months earlier at the Humane Society. Were we creating another episode for her to question whether to trust humans?

The surgery was a success, both eyes had new lenses. Following the cataract surgery Becky was to receive daily eye drops, of two medications, each administered separately. She still tried to avoid receiving these drops, but the resistance slowly declined, as her trust in us increased. But Becky would require eye drops in both eyes daily for the rest of her life. Every day when the eye drop bottle came out, she knew what to expect and tried to avoid it, but overtime her resistance declined.

In addition, we needed to limit her activity until the lenses were fully healed. But, after several weeks, one of the newly implanted lenses came loose, requiring surgery to reattach the lens, another opportunity for her to distrust humans. Fortunately, she handled the second surgery better than the first and her confidence continued to grow.

Several weeks after her cataract repair surgery, at a follow up visit to the ophthalmologist, Becky was given the approval to return to a normal active life. She went on to train with Bonnie and to compete in a number of different dog sports -- obedience, rally, and even agility, where she excelled. The Bonnie-Becky team had developed into a trusting relationship.

Possibly the proudest of their accomplishments was in agility, which is an event where the handler directs the dog through an obstacle course. The pieces of equipment includes things like tunnels the dog runs through, dog walks which is a 12 inch wide board, 20 feet in length, elevated 4-feet off the ground, that dogs walk over and tires hung 20-inches in the air that dogs jump through. For a once blind dog, these were pretty amazing feats. Our ophthalmologist surgeon was so excited with her progress and accomplishment he used a picture of Becky jumping through an elevated tire obstacle for the home page of his web site. We call Becky our medical marvel because her eye problems, frequent veterinary visits, eye drops and other medications, however this was just the beginning of her illnesses and injuries.

Success is not forever; Failure is not fatal.

At age 10, she had a gum disease requiring dental surgery and once again she was subjected to canine veterinarian office visits. Anesthetics, painful surgeries, recoveries, and Becky continued to trust us. How much do you enjoy visits to your dentist? Have you ever had oral surgery or periodontal work on your gums? It is painful and the recovery is very uncomfortable. Yet through it all, Becky continued to trust us.

At age 11, Becky tore her right rear leg ACL, this to requiring more surgery, post-surgery leg immobilization, then the introduction to canine rehabilitation treatment similar to human physical therapy treatments. Anyone who has had post-surgery PT might have some unkind words to say about it. Becky was asked to get into machines and equipment for her rehab and she continued to trust we were doing the right things for her.

At age 12, she had a stroke. This did not look like a good situation. Once again, more veterinary visits rehabilitation treatments and other appointments. By this time, Becky's trust in her pack, both humans and dogs, was secure and she believed everything we were doing was for her own good. While experiencing and recovering from a stroke, ACL tear, and extensive dental work, Becky trusted her pack members, never acting defensive toward other dogs or people.

Becky taught us about trust and perseverance, the many set-backs which had happened in her life were just speed bumps as she kept moving forward. Every time it seemed all was good in her life, she was faced with another challenge. And through it all, she never stopped trying and never stopped trusting.

PHARMACEUTICAL SALES

My first job out of college was as a pharmaceutical sales person. I sold respiratory products and my sales territory was primarily located at a very prestigious, "ivory tower" medical community including several large university associated hospitals. This was one of the five largest research-oriented medical institutions in the US and was known for conducting extensive medical research. The institution also took great pride in providing excellent training for physicians educated in a wide variety of specialties. These were the people creating procedures, techniques, and products of the future. To be on staff as a cardiologist, pulmonologist or other specialty you needed to be on top of your profession. These are the specialists who are first to know about new products and techniques.

If a general practitioner refers a patient to one of these specialists, the patient is expected to receive the care and medications not available to a general practitioner.

It is easy to dislike someone you don't know.

Such specialists found the products presented, by a sales representatives as jaded commercials from large corporations. They did not trust anything these sales people would tell them. They were not about to trust a non-MD salesperson to offer anything of value. In my territory, most physicians did not find any value in meeting with a pharmaceutical sales representative, so they didn't. It was considered a waste of their time.

My employer did not accept the "no sales" representative policies of the physician practices which constituted most of my territory, as an acceptable excuse for me not to see these physicians. Pharmaceutical companies employ sales people to present their products to the physicians in their territory. Telling your boss the doctors won't see sales representatives is not a viable excuse.

To keep my job, I needed to get in front of the highly influential pulmonary group. Numerous attempts resulted in the customary refusals. Like every other office in town, the staff was well trained to turn down every sales rep entering their office. But I was still getting pressure from my boss to see these specialists.

**Selling does not begin until you have heard "NO"
at least 7 times.**

The normal method of meeting with physicians, as established in the industry, was not going to work in my territory. I needed to do something different to get in front of these physicians. I started by trying to learn about the physician specialists from the office staff. For instance, I learned the youngest practitioner of the most influential pulmonary practice, liked to speak at medical education meetings. The office staff reluctantly shared some of his speaking locations, times and dates. I am sure they did not believe I would attend any of these events. It might not have been face-to-face but I could at least see what he looked like and get in front of him in the audience at these programs.

This was also a good experience for me as a young, naive sales person to learn more about the patient care of the diseases for the products I sold. It was an evening program, a distance from the university setting, in a rural community. Since most people prefer to sit in the rear of the room, I took a seat in the front row, right in front of the podium. It was a very worthwhile investment of time, since I learned the products he used, why, and when he used them. It was a great learning experience, so I continued attending his programs -- from the 6 a.m. Monday grand rounds to the Friday evening residence programs.

Persistence Overcomes Resistance

After several months of sitting in the front row, as close to the podium as possible, for as many of his programs I could attend, the young physician approached me at the conclusion of his presentation asking "Who are you?" This was the moment I had been dreaming would happen. I told him my name, employer and products I represented. I then went on to explain, his office practice had a policy of not speaking with sales representative, which means attending these programs is the only way I was able to speak with him.

My response took him by surprise, but he was caught between being flattered and laughing. The young specialist was very entertained I would attend so many of his presentations and he seemed to feel obligated to give me some of his time. After this conversation, I continued to attend his programs, and after each program the doctor gave me more of his time. After so many of his presentations, where I had taken copious notes and built a thorough knowledge of his prescribing habits, I scripted challenging, purposeful, open-ended questions to ask him. I got the impression our conversations were stimulating for the young doctor.

A medical practice, like any business, depends on referrals to obtain patients. Pulmonary specialists receive their referrals from general practitioners and internal medicine specialists. To grow his practice, the young specialist needed to establish a reputation with potential referral sources. Knowing the young doctor liked speaking at education programs and he did so sometimes without compensation, I had an "in." The company I worked for supported medical continuing education programs by paying speaking physicians with honorariums. I received approval from my manager to offer the young physician an opportunity to speak for us. I made him the offer that my company would be interested to compensate him for some of his presentations. My offer was received with interest and skepticism. He was still not sure if he could trust me, but after assuring him he was under no obligation to talk about my company's products, he agreed.

The young doctor was a very good speaker, had great platform skills and was humorous. His trust toward me was beginning to develop, but I still did not have access to him in his office. I don't think he wanted his partners to know he was talking with a big pharma sales person.

But we did spend time together before and after his speaking programs, which is where I was able to present research articles concerning my products. These conversations led to discussions regarding medications, which were still in the research phase, some of which were manufactured by my company. Because what separates a specialist from a generalist is the access to new medications, procedures, and information, he was very interested to learn anything new, especially any opportunities to participate as a Beta test site for a new product my company was developing.

It was not typical protocol for a sales person to initiate test site locations; there are designated departments and staff at any pharmaceutical company to handle such responsibilities. My first inquiry resulted in a very quick response, NO. I worked with my boss, then my boss's boss and then his boss to build my case. I was able to connect the young specialist with upper management in my company, which ultimately led to the opportunity for his practice to participate as a Beta test site for a bronchodilator in the final stages of testing.

As a participant, the practice would be required to do a lot of documentation. This meant more work for his administrative staff to track patients and the effects of the medicine. But when he introduced the opportunity to the other members of his group practice, it put the younger partner in a new light. The senior partners were understandably skeptical and concerned, because they did not trust any sales people, but they were very interested. Because the young doctor had begun to trust me, I was introduced to the other partners in the practice. Participating in the Beta studies was a lot of work for the physicians and their staff, and there were challenges, but I was always honest about what I could and could not do.

People buy from people

The senior member of this practice was chief of ICU and head of hospital staff grand rounds (which is a teaching experience where senior member of medical staff use case studies to provide innovative diagnostic and treatment techniques). Along with the younger members of the practice, they approached me for some help with his grand rounds program after hospital administration made financial cut backs in the monies for the weekly program. This was more proof; not only did the younger member of the practice trusted me, but now the eldest member, who was highly respected among hospital staff, I felt he, too, was beginning to trust me.

It was interesting to learn hospital politics of administration vs. physicians. I worked within the ethics of the physician's and administration's policies to make the chief of grand rounds look good. I was now trusted by the entire practice and was no longer considered a sales person but rather a problem solver. In confidence, the chief of grand rounds shared the story with physicians of similar hospital leadership status, which then opened opportunities for me to meet with senior members of other specialists practices such as cardiology and oncology whose patient care offices also had no sales representative policies.

Developing this trust opened additional opportunities for me.

On a Sunday afternoon, I received a phone call from the young physician asking if I would be willing to meet with him and his partners the following week to present my knowledge of new, soon-to-be released, pulmonary medication. I explained the product was not manufactured by my company, but rather by a competitor. He said his partners were aware of this, but felt my company might have access to information on our competitor's new product, which might not be found in medical journals.

He then said they had always found me to be objective and trustworthy. This is when the trust I had developed with the doctors in this practice became a sustained resource for them. A time to meet

259

was set and I am sure you know what I did during the short time I had until our meeting, a lot of study and many phone calls to my corporate office. The product manager's and research department at my company's corporate office were a wealth of information helping me to prepare a presentation and field the physician's questions.

Stanford Marshmallow Experiment

In 1972 at Stanford University, Walter Mischel conducted the Marshmallow experiment, using a group of over 600 children aged 4-6 as his subjects. Each child was asked to sit at a table in a room free of distractions and was given one marshmallow treat on a small plate. The child was then told he would receive an additional marshmallow if he could refrain from eating the first marshmallow until the experimenter returned (about fifteen to twenty minutes later). A few children ate the marshmallow as soon as the researcher left the room, but of all those who attempted to delay; about 30% were successful in waiting for the full time allotment and earned the second marshmallow.

In 1988, Mischel conducted a follow up to his studies by investigating what had become of his original study participants, finding some startling discoveries. Children who were able to defer gratification were described by their parents as being more assertive, confident, and more academically competent than those who were unable to wait for a second marshmallow. In the second follow up study in 1990, the ability to delay gratification correlated with higher SAT scores. Children who could wait for the second marshmallow scored an average of 1262 (out of 1800) on the SAT. Those who ate their marshmallow early had an average score of 1052. In addition, those possessing the deferred gratification trait prove to have higher IQ scores, lower body fat, and a higher sense of self-worth, than those in need of immediate gratification.

Immediate vs Deferred Gratification

Building trust is a long term commitment in most cases providing little if any immediate feedback. Attempting to pursue large, long term goals, such as building trust, often requires putting aside immediate gratification of small short rewards. The lack of immediate gratification can become an obstacle, often sabotaging efforts to the attainment of long term goals. Those possessing the ability to stay motivated while pursuing a goal which does not provide immediate gratification is referred to as deferred gratification.

Though a genetic link has not been found, it appears deferred gratification is an innate trait at birth. Those who possess the trait of deferred gratification tend to be most likely to implement long term goals throughout their entire lives.

Deferred gratification is a desirable trait, but very few people can work long term in pursuit of a major goal without some reward or feedback.

Having a goal of obtaining a college diploma is often referred to as deferred gratification, it is a major, long term goal, taking years to attain. But it also provides opportunities to receive more frequent rewards such as receiving a test score, single class grade and credits toward the much larger goal of a Bachelor's Degree. It is a matter of reprograming our focus from a long term goal to many shorter term goals providing more immediate feedback.

Earlier in this chapter I stated the selling doesn't begin till you hear the word "NO" seven times. This is another example of deferred gratification. Most sales people will give up and move to another customer long before they have heard seven no's. If the customers purchasing potential has been qualified as sizable, thus highly worth pursuing, it may take years of work without rewards to sell such customers. Such customers require a major investment of time and effort with little rewards over long periods of time.

Similar to training a new skill or pursuing a long term goal, deferred gratification is most successfully accomplished when broken down into small short term accomplishments which can provide intrinsic or extrinsic rewards.

When training a new exercise or attempting to program behavior we need to utilize immediate, repetitive, frequent rewards. This immediate gratification stimulates the recipient's attention toward the vehicle providing these rewards. The more frequent and immediate the rewards are given, the greater opportunity for attention. This is very useful in attaining short term small goals. These small successes are important to moving forward on long-term larger goals. By re-directing attention to shorter accomplishments rather than a massive long-term goal, motivation becomes easier. Frequent small reward opportunities keeping us motivated and moving forward to our larger long-term goal.

Sales

Long-term success in sales requires consistency and dependability, which are components of trust. When customers trust a salesperson, the customer will look for reasons to support the sales person products or services, thus selling themselves, on the sales person's product or service. Due to the level of trust in the sales person, customers will look for ways to include the salespersons products or service in their company's purchases. Highly productive sales people distinguish themselves as problem solvers or sustained resources with their customer's. Problem solvers and sustained resources seldom need to close a sale, because the customer will close themselves. Those who go into sales for fast success are doomed to fail because building relationships and trust takes time.

The most effective salesperson any company has is a satisfied customer. Most sales result from word of mouth, one friend telling another friend; or one family member telling another family member about their satisfaction. A friend or family member who has no vested interest in the purchase decision is considered by the potential buyer as trustworthy and believable.

Trust

I find it very sad in our current world of immediate gratification, where people do not understand the importance of developing trust. Trust should not be something which is quick or easy to obtain.

How often have you heard the words "trust me"?

Why should I trust anyone?

Lack of trust among pack members leads to reduced productivity. Pack members do not work to their potential when they do not trust other members of their pack.

Failure increases the frequency of distrust.

In contrast, success encourages trust.

Trust means putting others needs in front of your own; which is not natural behavior unless you are a true born leader. Most informal leaders work in the best interest of the pack.

If you have built the trust in others, you have probably also proven to those same people you have integrity, ethics, and morals

Trust is an intangible which cannot be measured with metrics. You cannot weigh it or count it or touch it. It is instead made up of many components. Trust is a conglomeration of many factors all coming together and staying together. No one element is more important than any of the others, so the order presented is random.

Consistency is important to building trust because it builds the foundation of knowing what can be expected. Those who produce a pattern of consistency establish a sense of dependability with others. With confidence, others have expectations of how you will react, regardless of whether the situation is stressful or cordial.

Respect is a building block to earning trust. It is hard to trust someone without respecting them and vice-versa. The two are tightly woven together.

Predictability, like consistency, helps build trust. Knowing what to expect of another pack member because it's been proven to be true multiple times, builds confidence among pack members.

Structure is found in the behavior and lives of people who earn trust.

Honesty is another component creating trust, there needs to be proof over a period of time.

Confidence is an outcome of trust. When you have confidence you also have earned trust.

Time, like consistency, is important to building trust because it builds the foundation on which others know what you stand for. When your values are put to the test over a long period of time, we learn what to expect and who can be trusted.

Trust is an everyday, long term commitment.

If you have earned the trust of others, it is because you have been proven to tell the truth, not once, but all of the time.

Trust neither comes easy nor often. But once you've built and earned it, trust is a special feeling.

Trust

Trust must be earned.

Trust improves with honest communication.

Trust does not come from words; it comes from actions.

Trust requires consistent behavior.

Trust is not a sometimes thing, it is an all-the-time thing.

Trust takes a long time to build.

And, when trust is lost it is very hard to regain!

How many people do you trust?

**Winning and losing are just short term consequences
to the long term goal; improvement**

Book "Top Dog"

Whether you think you can or think you can't ----you're right.

Henry Ford

Chapter Thirteen

Dusty

Our Golden Retriever Rescue Organization was asked to help with three dogs which had been confiscated from an abusive owner. All three dogs were thin, malnourished, and had intestinal worms. Even worse they all tested positive for heart worm. Their coats were short thin hair, very brittle, and dull. One of the dogs was red in color and was in the worst condition of the three. Her right front leg was badly damaged from what appeared to have been a wire or cable wrapped around it for extended period of time. There were grooves worn into her canine teeth which seemed to indicate she had been biting and pulling on the wire attempting to escape the wires grasp.

This weak, sickly looking red headed Golden Retriever was given the name Dusty. Dusty walked on three legs due to the damage done to her front right leg. The first efforts of our Golden Retriever Rescue group were to rehab the injured front leg with swim therapy, but those exercises did not improve circulation or strength. The decision was made to amputate her leg. Due to her malnourished weakened condition there was a strong possibility Dusty would not survive the operation, but there weren't any other options.

The operation took place with amazing results, Dusty survived the amputation. Post-surgery most of her time was spent kenneled recovering from the recent trauma. Due to the effects of surgery and medications she mostly slept. Sleep and rest was what she needed because he suture wounds from her amputation were still healing.

Dusty was still bony, with a short brittle coat, rat like tail, and very weak. She had difficulty standing and walking on her three legs and was only able to take two or three clumsy, pogo like bouncy, awkward steps at a time before stopping to take a break, panting, and catching her breath. It was strenuous for her just to walk a few steps.

Her breathing was riled and labored. She still had heart worms and was very weak, but needed to begin receiving heart worm treatment. The treatment for heart worm was daily doses of arsenic extending over six weeks. Even for a healthy dog such a treatment severely weakens the patient, and a percentage of these patients die. Once again, the chance of this weak red head surviving the heart worm treatment did not look very good.

About the same time she began receiving heart worm treatment it was in her best interest to move her out of kennel life and into a foster home. This is when the next step of her rehab process began; we took Dusty in as a foster. How would this poor pathetic animal adapt to her new pack. At the time we took on Dusty as a foster we had four dogs in our pack, three of the four were rescues with low self-confidence. All four of the current pack members were physically healthy and strong. They had daily activities such as agility training, dog walks, chasing tennis balls, etc. keeping them lean, muscular and fit. Since they were so much stronger than Dusty we were concerned in her current weak condition, Dusty could easily be injured by any bumping or rough house dog play with her new pack.

We cautiously introduced Dusty to each of our existing pack members to protect her from any harm. Our belief was this weak three legged dog needed to be protected from the possible active play of our dog pack. But instead, Dusty was welcomed by all of the dogs as a confident leader. The original four pack member immediately through their own intuitive ability recognized Dusty's condition. They were respectful of her and with wagging tails were glad to meet her. Even though the original members of the pack could physically run circles around Dusty, she was so respected by all of the other dogs in the pack looking to her as their new leader. Dusty had not just been accepted as a member of the Hornfisher pack of four, now five, but she had established herself with them as their Alpha. How could this weak, sickly, new entry to the pack, get so much respect from these strong healthy original pack members? True confidence and leadership are not learned traits; they are characteristics a dog is born with, which could be seen in Dusty.

Dusty was still very sickly, and there were no guarantees she would live or for how long. As with every new foster which came into our house we evaluated the situation and created plan for her recovery. Creating the best diet and dosing to strengthen bones, build muscle, and grow some coat. There was also the need for exercise to build her endurance without exhausting her. When we started, she was learning how to walk on just three legs. She would take two or three clumsy, bounce steps then stop panting and trying to catch her breath. She was still taking heart worm medications which took a lot of her strength. Dusty made daily trips outdoors for short exercise sessions. We started trying to walk 20-30 feet as she would pogo stick bouncing on her left front leg followed by a couple short steps with her back legs. Then stop to catch her breath. She would again take another step the same way. Dusty demonstrated her strong drive to survive.

Over the course of the next six months we slowly progressed to the point where each left leg pogo bounce moved farther forward with less height. Thus each step was becoming more efficient, using less energy to progress further forward. We went from 20-30 foot walks to 50 yard walks up and down the drive way. The next step was to make a lap around our property line which was about ¼ mile. This would be more challenging because the ground was not as level and included some hills. We were now four months into the rehab process; she had survived the heart worm treatment, and was now capable of building muscle and endurance. Dusty would make daily walks of one lap around our property or about ¼ mile, once per day, then twice per day. When we got up to two laps around the property twice a day, Dusty was ready to begin running.

After living with us for a year Dusty had mastered the skill of running on three legs. Because running requires longer strides, her running gait was smoother, less pogo bouncy than her slow walking. Dusty looked more comfortable running and appeared to have better body balance than she did slow walking. Like riding a bike, the faster the bike is moving, the smoother, easier it is to balance the ride. One day while playing tennis ball chase with four other dogs, we had several neighbors watching the entertainment, after several retrieves one of the spectators made the comment "do you realize one of those dogs only has three legs". This realization created even greater interest in the crowd with cheers when she would out run the others to be the first to retrieve the thrown ball.

With everything she had to endure Dusty never showed signs of giving up. Whatever we asked of her, taking medication, exercise, going to the vet or anything else she always gave her best effort to respond to our requests. She readily accepted entering a pack of four new dogs and was instantly accepted as the pack leader.

Dusty's rehab of exercise, medications, and a balanced diet had transformed a pathetic sickly dog into a beautifully red silky coated healthy looking dog. Dusty had made a very successful recovery, and she was getting stronger every day. Through the whole process she continued to be viewed by her pack members as their leader. She never growled, snapped or had a fight with any of the member of our pack, it was just simply accepted she was their leader.

This amazing dog, as weak as she was she was always friendly. After all she had endured, she continued to like people, and responded to human requests. Dusty's natural disposition was of a very confident dog.

While Dusty was a member of our pack she remained the Alpha dog.

Even at her weakest, sickest time in life Dusty possessed an aura of confidence which other dogs recognized. Her confidence and leadership was evident from the time she was first rescued from an abusive owner; Dusty seemed to be the leader and protector of the other two dogs she was found with. After their rescue the three were separated and placed in different foster homes. From what we have heard the other two dogs continued to be submissive and much slower to trust humans. Dusty was a very special dog displayed true leadership qualities.

One year after joining our pack Dusty had built up her strength and stamina. She looked great. Dusty had proven she had the right stuff to start a career in sales. So it was time for her to start traveling with me on road trips making sales calls with customers and business meetings. Dusty was one of the best sales "people" I have ever had the pleasure to work with. She could charm the toughest customer. When I made sales calls with her we would walk in, everyone would faun all over her, she would simply be Dusty with a wagging tail, bright sparkly eyes, enjoying the attention and petting from anyone and everyone. When I took her to work trade show exhibits she understood to hang out in the display booth and greet customers. Even when I would walk away talking with customers she stayed in the booth. With her by my side I believe I could have run for political office. She even enjoyed staying in hotel rooms. Regardless of the new challenge facing her, Dusty would confidently take it on without hesitation. She confidently pursued each new situation with an eagerness to learn.

Confidence is the foundation for achievement

Her talents were observed by a customer of mine who owned a prosthetic company. It took a lot of persuasion over several months, including him and his family visiting our home to spend time with Dusty. As usual Bonnie had accurately sized up the situation, Dusty would be better off with three people, six hands to pet her, than being one of five dogs competing for two people, four hands to pet her. Her life turned out great. She spent the rest of her life going to work every day at a prosthetic business. Every day she is receiving a lot of attention from patients both as a relaxing friend to pet in the waiting room or as a motivator in the gait lab with her three legged gait or inspiration in the exam room for her positive attitude. Yes, Dusty became gainfully employed with a full time job. Her home life is also great, where she is allowed on the new sofa as well as any other furniture. Dusty even learned the most efficient, three legged method, of leaping onto and sliding off of high furniture.

MABEL AND ANTHONY

My earliest memory of my grandmother was visiting her in the hospital after she had experienced a massive cerebral hemorrhage. The stroke left her entire right hemisphere paralyzed. This took place back in the mid 1950's where the care and rehab for a stroke was a lots of bed rest. After several days in the hospital the doctors told my grandmother the right side of her body was permanently paralyzed and she would never walk again. They went on to explain she needed to learn how to use a wheelchair. Mabel did not take this news real well. I was not in the room, but have been told even though Mabel had always been right handed, which was now paralyzed, she was very effective expressing her dissatisfaction with the doctors prognosis, by throwing a water glass, with her left hand, at the physicians, as they hastily retreated from the room, with water still in the glass, it shattering into many pieces hitting the hall way floor. This was just the start of a turbulent relationship between Mabel and the attending physicians. She made it known she would walk again.

I guess the physicians feared more water glass projectile attacks so they arranged for an intermediary to discuss an armistice. Several days following the doctors telling Grandma Mabel of her future fate, a gentleman by the name of Anthony showed up at her hospital room. Anthony did not waste any time making an examination of Mabel's physical condition. He then had a conversation with Mabel, stating "I can make you walk". What! The doctors, the authorities, you know the people in white coats with big titles, said she would not walk again. Who is this Anthony, claiming to possess the magic which would make Mabel walk again, especially after physicians said she would not? Is he selling false promises? Mabel liked Anthony and his belief in her. Mabel was a fighter, who had things to do with her life. She believed in Anthony and she followed his directions to prove those doctors wrong. Anthony had given Mabel a vision of what she could do and how she could prove those doctors wrong.

Mabel was not the type of person to sit inactive; she had things to do with her life. We learned Anthony was a Certified Prosthetist-Orthotist; he made braces and prosthetic body parts. Anthony was true to his words, he made a leg brace for Grandma Mabel. Anthony explained to Mabel's her new brace was just the start of the rehabilitation process. He told her she had to work with Physical

273

Therapy to learn to use this new brace. The Physical Therapy sessions were grueling, taxing Mabel's strength. There were many failures, but, she was determined to walk. She started with a great deal of physical support by physical therapist holding her up as she tried to move her legs. Then she moved to parallel bars where she could use her left arm to help support herself while Physical Therapist provided additional support. The Physical Therapists were very demanding, and Mabel used some colorful words to describe their therapy sessions.

After many weeks of working hard, good days and bad days, with many set-backs, Mabel was walking between the parallel bars with minimal use of her hand. Mabel believed Anthony was a miracle worker. He told her she would walk and here she was walking. She made sure all of those wheelchair-touting doctors saw her walking. Mable admired Anthony the rest of her life. She spoke of him as if he had come from heaven.

This was just the start of her rehab; she had to re-learn a lot of daily activity skills. Paralyzed on her right side, her dominate side, required she learn to write with her left hand, as well as, re-learning with the left hand to do many other daily activities this took the expertise of an Occupational Therapist. Her speech had also been affected by the stroke, once again with the help of Speech Therapist she had developed skills to regain her ability to talk. All of these re-learning events involved many failures and setbacks, which were frustrating and angering. Every set back just fueled her drive to work harder.

The only real failure; is not trying

But she had her goals and persisted in her quest to resume pre-stroke activities. As these many different physical skills improved Mabel was moving closer to getting back into her previously active life. After being discharged from the hospital she went back to the active life she had always enjoyed. Mable had always been an active volunteer in her church. She organized a women's group to make chocolate candies which the church would sell to raise money. She wasn't able to personally make the chocolates but she sure could recruit more than enough people to do the physical tasks. One handed telephone calling was time consuming, this was the era of rotary dial phones, so with her one functioning left hand, she would laboriously dial and call on her volunteer friends.

When at church she was meeting with people and enlisting them to become volunteers. She did not stop with just chocolates to raise money; she also organized Friday evening fish fry's at the church which also raised money. All of the work was done by volunteers who had been organized by Mabel. She also organized Sunday breakfasts which took place between the early and late morning church services. All of these activities required people to purchase supplies, set up tables and chairs, prepare the food, clean up, and return everything to the original condition. These activities involved many people, with a variety of talents, which was organized by this semi-paralyzed woman.

Mabel may not have possessed the physical skill of the people she put to work on her projects, but for some reason people wanted to work for her. Because Mabel had confidence in her and her goals, others could easily sense and wanted to follow. She inspired trust and confidence in others who wanted to follow and fulfill her goals.

Another important memory I have of Grandma Mabel was the importance to always be properly dressed. She enjoyed a new hat or new dress. She took great pride in her appearance. It might take her a long time to get dressed using just one hand, but it was always important to look nice.

Throughout the rest of her life, like all of us, Mabel had challenges and set-backs but she just kept motoring ahead.

"I have not failed 1,000 times; I have learned 1,000 materials that are not good material for a filament."

Thomas Edison

It was many years later I got a job in the orthotic and prosthetic industry and had the good fortune to find Mabel's old friend, Anthony. He now had taken his small prosthetic and orthotic company, with just one location, which I remembered Grandma Mabel visiting, to have work done on her leg brace, and built his business into a large orthotic and prosthetic practice. With thirty-six locations, Anthony had added durable medical equipment to the services he offered in these offices. Then he expanded to provide mail order diabetic and respiratory supplies.

Anthony never stopped working on his many ideas; he also founded the Athletes with Disability Hall of Fame, which had an annual awards banquet. With his love of sports he didn't just watch events on television; he met and developed friendships with local professional sports celebrities. It was these celebrities and friends helping Anthony develop his ideas to reality creating philanthropic projects. Anthony was very successful getting these local sports heroes and celebrities to emcee and participate in his annual banquets to raise money for philanthropic projects. Local sports celebrities were often seen in his office visiting with Anthony.

Like Mabel, Anthony was very successful motivating others to fulfill his vision. Anthony possessed the natural leadership which motivated others to follow. He was very successful building a large orthotic and prosthetic practice as well as many philanthropic projects. Anthony continued to work six-days per week till his death at age 91.

We all have handicaps; some are more obvious than others.

So what does Anthony have to do with Dusty? Anthony had lost both of his legs, below the knee, in a childhood accident. But due to his self-confidence, determination, and naturally born leadership, he simply made things happen. Anthony wore prosthetic devices on both legs. Prior to starting his own business he had turned down for many jobs because he was a "cripple". As soon as a prospective employer; or when he did land a job; and the employer learned he wore prosthetic legs, they terminate his employment. Like both Dusty and Mabel, Anthony never felt sorry for himself nor did he let his handicap or failures stop him from achieving goals. All three experienced many set-backs and failures in life. But most important all three are examples of natural leaders who attract the support of others. People want to follow nature leaders.

Confidence

Confidence is very important to leadership. People and dogs sense confidence and like to follow those with confidence. True confident, for the most part, is a trait people or dogs are born with.

Confident dogs do not bite, growl, snap or bark in an attacking mode. Confident dogs greet new people and other dogs as friends. Confidence is an amazing trait. Those who possess confidence are constantly trying to learn new things. Confident dogs or people look at failure as just another adventure in life. When they fail or make a mistake they are quick to accept responsibility and move on. Those who have confidence view failure as a learning experience. Confident dogs will walk by a barking; growling dog without reacting because they recognize the barking dog is simply scared. Confident dogs do not waste their time reacting to the issues of scared dogs, who's barking and/or growling is an attempt to intimidate.

Dogs lacking confidence are likely to greet new dogs and/or people with fear, snapping, barking, lunging and biting because they are scared. They are fearful and are trying to scare away anything new. These are usually the Omega's of the dog pack. They are the lowest member of a pack hierarchy. Humans are the same way; those who greet others with rude, insulting, nasty comments are scared and insecure. Those who have to constantly attack others rationalizing such behavior to be a display of confidence, misunderstand the definition of arrogance and confidence.

Insecure humans fear new things; they are the omegas, bottom of the pack. They like to keep everything around themselves consistent, and are not likely to try anything new. They like to use tried and tested routines. These are people who fear failure. When they make mistakes they retract and obsess over the mistake rather than appreciate the learning opportunity it has presented. Because their self-confidence is shallow, scared people often have difficulty getting beyond any failure or mistakes they make. They often fear more making a mistake than to learn or experience something new.

Success is not forever; failure is not fatal.

Insecure individuals surround themselves with barriers to keep others away. They create work areas which look more like bunkers than offices. They like to put artificial obstacles in places to keep others at a distance. Confident people create work areas providing openness and few barriers so communication is promoted. The fewer barriers separating people one from another, the greater opportunity for open communication.

If you never made a mistake; you have never learned.

For those pack members who are not born with the confidence of an Alpha can build confidence through the use of a variety of techniques. Developing confidence in those who are born without it is referred to as learned confidence, because it is a result of learning how to become more confident, in particular activities of life. Throughout this book I have tried to demonstrate some techniques to help develop more confidence in yourself or teammates. Activities such as training, consistent behavior, goal setting, respect, and proofing are useful methods toward building confidence.

Failure

People without confidence respond to failures or mistakes as a terrible thing. They carry the scars of past mistakes or failures as reasons not to challenge themselves a second time. Those who do not have confidence are fearful of doing the wrong thing, so they want to stay in a safe zone which they have followed in the past and not gotten into trouble. Often when a person lacking confidence makes a mistake or has a failure they look for someone else to blame. Fear of failure is a constant companion of lower tier pack members. In contrast confident people view failure or mistakes as an opportunity to learn.

"The only real mistake is the one from which we learn nothing."
Henry Ford

The real leaders in life are those who possess the confidence to follow their passions fulfilling their beliefs. Failure for these people is a wonderful opportunity to learn something new. Confident people own their mistakes or failures. They find failure or mistakes as an educational experience to be appreciated. They also realize if you have never failed or made a mistake, you have never learned a thing. Confident people are always looking for new things to learn, so when they fail or make a mistake they inquisitively pursue the opportunity to learn something new.

Discrimination

Like Anthony, many leaders have experienced discrimination. Franklin D. Roosevelt, 32 President of the United States and only president to be elected four terms, overcame adversity and experienced discrimination due to his polio which he contracted at age 39 years old. Early in the 20th century, before the American Disabilities Act, people with physical disabilities experienced discrimination. FDR learned first-hand people with physical disabilities were not allowed to sit in the same area of restaurant or trains as "normal people". Having grown up in an affluent family FDR spent the first 38 years of life distance from such prejudice. After spending ten years learning to live with his paralysis his personal experience with discrimination gave him empathy for others experiencing discrimination, not only due to physical disabilities but also such things as race and religious.

When FDR became President of United States he worked hard creating programs to fight discrimination. Similar to FDR Anthony experience job discrimination due to his artificial legs, and used his experience to create programs to help others. Great leaders, like FDR and Anthony, work to better the lives of others.

Struggles

Whether it is called struggles, hardships, failures or setbacks in life, such events are commonly found in the lives of great leaders. Orville and Wilbur Wright battled depression and family health issues but were not deterred from their passion to fly.

Success is going from failure to failure without losing enthusiasm.

Winston Churchill

Winston Churchill flunked sixth grade, spent his life dealing with bipolar depression, dyslexia, speech impediment, attention deficit hyperactive disorder, and loosing multiple elections. Then at the darkest hours in England's history, as Nazi Germany had Blitz Krieged through Europe, Winston Churchill became Prime Minister of England. England looked like German's next easy conquest. With confidence, Churchill rallied his country to successfully defend their country. Throughout his entire life, Churchill had many struggles, so he was prepared for such a challenge.

Like other great leaders Abraham Lincoln experienced many struggles in his life. Here is a list of the events in Abraham Lincoln life:

Mother died (at age 9)

Failed in business (at age 22)

Defeated for legislature (at age 23)

Failed in business (at age 24)

Elected to legislature (at age 25)

Sweetheart died (at age 26)

Suffered a nervous breakdown (at age 27)

Defeated for speaker (at age 29)

Defeated for elector (at age 31)

Elected to congress (at age 35)

Son died (at age 41)

Defeated for senate (at age 46)

Defeated for Vice-Presidency (at age 47)

Defeated for senate (at age 49)

Elected President of the United States (at age 51)

Lincoln took office as the President of the United States in the midst of a civil war. He unwaveringly dedicated himself to holding the United States together. Like Churchill his life was filled with many struggles, the civil war was another challenge in his life. FDR took office three years into the country's worst depression, with record high unemployment creating programs to pull the country back together. Winston Churchill became Prime Minister of England as Nazi

Germany had rolled through Europe and preparing to invade England. All of these were dismal situations, which would be overwhelming to most; all three of these people had become accustom to difficult situations. The hardships and struggles they had dealt with throughout life prepared them for such overwhelming challenges. Leadership is about facing adversity with confidence, creating a vision and motivating others towards achievement. Great Leaders learn from their struggles and continue moving forward.

Leaders create a vision for others to follow

On May 25, 1961, John F. Kennedy stood before Congress and proclaimed "This nation should commit itself to achieving the goal, before the decade is out, of landing a man on the moon and returning him safely to the Earth." He did not say we would *like* to; nor did he say it would be a worthwhile project to *look into*; nor did he say we will *try* to accomplish. John F. Kennedy stated the USA would complete this task by the end of the decade. He spoke confidently creating a vision, that made others believe, we as a nation, would make happen and then he told them when it would happen.

Leaders create visions for others to believe will happen and then the followers make his vision happen.

The "HOW" is easy when you have a "WHY."

When the speech was made, NASA had just been created. Even more remarkable, the USA had not been able to launch any type of rocket of any size without it self-destructing.

But, at the time the USSR was far ahead of the USA in the space race and John F. Kennedy needed to do something to get things moving forward. And fast. He needed to mobilize the entire country on a single-focused event, which was tangible, measureable, and understandable by every American. Nothing motivates people like competition. Which is just exactly what JFK did, he threw down the challenge to the rest of the world, including what the USA was going to do and when. Great leaders confidently provide a vision; they are smart enough to allow others, who possess the specific talents and skill with the freedom and creativity to figure out **HOW** the actual project will be accomplished.

JFK did not talk about what type of rocket booster would be used, nor did he explain in details what the vehicle would look like. He didn't create the idea of stages of development through separate programs such as Mercury, Gemini, and Apollo. He had no idea **HOW** it was going to happen, which was up to the scientists, engineers, and business people. What he gave Americans was a clear vision of **WHAT** needed to be accomplished and **WHEN**. Leaders are good at motivating their followers toward a common goal and keeping them focused to achieve that goal.

Leaders have visions and inspire others to accomplish those visions.

Dogs like people, want someone to believe and follow. The vast majority of any population wants to follow a leader; they want someone to look to for direction. Leaders provide a vision to direct the efforts of their followers. Without this vision followers will work independent thereby reducing the effectiveness of the entire group. A pack or group focused on a common goal will accomplish far more than will the same individuals working separately without a common vision.

Humans follow confident leaders.

Anthony created a vision for Mable, I can make you walk. He did not tell her all of the details. He did not complicate the message with all of the agonizing days working in PT. Nor did he tell her all of the failures she would have to endure to accomplish her goal. He gave her a vision; she had to figure out how to make it happen.

The most respected leaders make decisions based on the greater benefits it will have for others. Great leaders put their egos aside and make decisions for the masses they serve rather than for personal gain. Great leaders instinctively do things to help others.

Great leaders make everyone else around them better.
Confident people look for ways to help others
Confident people take pride in their appearance
Confident people are aware of what they put into their body
Confident people take pride in their health
Confident people own their decisions and behavior
Confident people walk with square shoulders and long strides
Confident people laugh often and easily
Confident people find ways to compliment others
Confident people are good listeners
Confident people like to learn new things
Confident people initiate conversations with strangers

**The worst things that happen in life
are often the best things.**

Struggle is Good!   I Want to Fly!

Once a little boy was playing outdoors and found a fascinating caterpillar. He carefully picked it up and took it home to show his mother. He asked his mother if he could keep it, and she said he could if he would take good care of it.

The little boy got a large jar from his mother and put plants to eat, and a stick to climb on, in the jar. Every day he watched the caterpillar and brought it new plants to eat.

One day the caterpillar climbed up the stick and started acting strangely. The boy worriedly called his mother who came and understood that the caterpillar was creating a cocoon. The mother explained to the boy how the caterpillar was going to go through a metamorphosis and become a butterfly.

The little boy was thrilled to hear about the changes his caterpillar would go through. He watched every day, waiting for the butterfly to emerge. One day it happened, a small hole appeared in the cocoon and the butterfly started to struggle to come out.

At first the boy was excited, but soon he became concerned. The butterfly was struggling so hard to get out! It looked like it couldn't break free! It looked desperate! It looked like it was making no progress!

The boy was so concerned he decided to help. He ran to get scissors, and then walked back (because he had learned not to run with scissors...). He snipped the cocoon to make the hole bigger and the butterfly quickly emerged!

As the butterfly came out the boy was surprised. It had a swollen body and small, shriveled wings. He continued to watch the butterfly expecting that, at any moment, the wings would dry out, enlarge and expand to support the swollen body. He knew that in time the body would shrink and the butterfly's wings would expand.

But neither happened!

The butterfly spent the rest of its life crawling around with a swollen body and shriveled wings.

It never was able to fly...

As the boy tried to figure out what had gone wrong his mother took him to talk to a scientist from a local college. He learned that the butterfly was **SUPPOSED** to struggle. In fact, the butterfly's struggle to push its way through the tiny opening of the cocoon pushes the fluid out of its body and into its wings. Without the struggle, the butterfly would never, ever fly. The boy's good intentions hurt the butterfly.

As you go through school, and life, keep in mind that struggling is an important part of any growth experience. In fact, it is the struggle that causes you to develop your ability to fly.

**It is not the title or job description;
It is what you do with it.**

Chapter Fourteen

Fred

Even though the name of this book is "How to Treat Your Employees Like a Dog", I have to include a cat. Fred was an amazing cat. Fred became part of our pack by his own choice. Pet Outfitters did not sell any live animals, instead providing a breeder referral program. When customers would come in expressing an interest to adopt a pet we would provide them with local breeder to contact for a dog. In addition, multiple times every year Pet Outfitters would hold a mobile adoption program in conjunction with a local animal shelter. The local shelter would bring dogs and cats in stacked wire crates on wheels. They would wheel the crate structures containing the animals into the store or on nice weather days, they would set up the crates in an area just outside the store entry. The program was advertised in advance to help improve the adoption numbers.

These adoptable animals arrive at our store overwhelmed by a morning of being re-crated into mobile stacked crates, which were then wheeled onto truck lift, secured in a panel truck, and transported some distance to our store. When they arrived at the Pet Outfitter parking lot they are wheeled off the truck and placed in the store. After such an experience most of these animals are stressed, scared or at the very least wary of all the changes. For this reason most of the animals typically spend their day at our store curled up in the rear of their crate. As customers walked by the crates, most all animals showed caution not interested to move toward the front of their crate.

On one of these occasions a black and white short hair cat was in one of the cages. His name was Fred and his reaction to the experience was anything but typical. Fred was at the front of his crate swing his front paw as customers passed by. It was as if he was trying to flag down those passing by to stop and visit. Fred especially took a liking to Bonnie. Anytime she got near his crate he began flirting by meowing and waving his front paws. Our store employees who observed his behavior believed he understood Bonnie was the store owner and a person of importance. We learned Fred had a sixth sense to size up situations and people.

Fred understood how to read people.

I am sure you already have the picture, Fred was quickly adopted. This was an easy decision. Fred made it very clear, we needed a store cat and he was born for this job. Fred was a very special cat, he was very confident. He could read other animal's demeanor, as friendly or predatory. From the moment he was rolled into the store Fred knew this was his new home. His confidence was very evident.

In addition, he was also very respectful. Fred understood his position in the pack. He appreciated the opportunity to be a member of the pack and saw the dogs as his equal. More importantly, the dogs in our pack respected Fred. He earned respect by his behavior. Fred was 12 pounds, compared to the dogs in our pack weighing 45-65 pounds each. Fred's front paws were de-clawed. Any one of the dogs could have easily crushed Fred at any time. But none of our dogs messed with Fred.

If Fred was asleep on a dog bed, none of the dogs ever challenged him for the bed. In the beginning Fred lived in the store making himself comfortable on the many dog beds, cat furniture or other items on display in the store. As time elapsed he became an integral part of our family and made frequent trips home. At home he exuded the same demeanor as he had in the store.

For example, if several members of the pack were playing in a room and Fred walked through, they would stop their rough housing and pay Fred the respect he so deserved as he slowly sauntered through the room to whatever chair, sofa, or dog bed he decided was calling his name. After Fred had comfortably situated himself, the dogs would return to the group play activities in the same location Fred had just passed through. It was as though Fred was Moses parting the Red Sea of dogs as he walked through the room. It is fascinating how he was not afraid of the much larger stronger members of his pack.

Even more interesting were the episodes when Fred decided he wanted to bless one of the dogs with his presence. We would observe one of our dogs lying on a dog bed, then Fred would slowly, confidently walk up to their restful position and lay down next to them. The dogs did not try to shoo him away, nor did they try to escape having to lie next to Fred. They appeared as if it was special recognition to have Fred share a dog bed with them. We also observed Fred's awareness of his pack members need for attention. If a pack member was ill, Fred instinctively perceived the issue, spending more time close to the weakened dog. This same behavior was observed when aging dogs were approaching their last days on earth; Fred seemed to stay close to them. He had a sense they were hurting and in need of some special attention. When these situations occurred Fred would clean the ailing pack mate coat, ears or face. I have said jokingly, if Fred begins to spend time with me, cleaning my face or ears, I needed to visit a doctor.

Fred understood how to help those in need.

Bonnie's daily routine would be to drive to Pet Outfitters in the morning with two or three dogs and Fred in the car. They would spend their days working the store. In the evening the pack would ride home together. So everyone one was gainfully employed in sales and customer service at the store. It was during those years of employment at the store where we learned more about Fred's ability to read people and animals behavior. There were times when Fred would disappear, not to be found, usually when a cat aggressive dog entered the store. Many times as hard as we would search the store to find him, he could not be found. Yet minutes after the departure of the threat, Fred would make himself reappear. He knew when to just disappear and for how long. Fred understood who he could trust and when to avoid any conflicts. His survival and success in life was his ability to help those who needed his help, surround himself with those who made him look good and avoid those who could do him harm.

Fred understood who to trust

Fred was the same with humans. He would select customers who he thought needed his help either to demonstrate the proper use of cat toys, the comforts of cat beds, or provide stress relief for those who he allowed to pet him. He also enjoyed helping customers when they laid their purses on the checkout counter, while they were paying, Fred would climb in their purse and take inventory or using his front paw to empty their purse item by item. This did not result in upset customers, but rather built a bond with Fred's new friend who would return many times again to visit the cat who liked their purse.

Since Fred appreciated all of the items we had, he felt it his responsibility to try out and test them all, including those in window displays. Such behavior resulted in passer-byers coming into the store to report they spotted a "live" cat in the store window. Since Fred spent most of his time in the display window lying on cat or dog furniture asleep, I am not sure how they knew he was alive. They may have been startled when what they thought was toy cat, moved.

Fred understood how to make others glad they met him.

On one occasion, we had a husband and wife couple come into the store and just walked around eyeing stacks of dog beds, then scanning the cat furniture. When asked by a store employee "how can I help you" their response was "just looking" and they continued to peruse. Finally, after time had elapsed and the couple sensed the staff were getting suspicious the woman said they were planning to have with lunch with our son at the restaurant across the parking lot, but he suggested we first visit Pet Outfitters to meet Fred, where is he?

Fred had the special ability to make Friends with humans, canines as well as felines.

MICHAEL

When entering an Italian restaurant on a Wednesday night, I was surprised to find it was crowded. It was middle of the week. Why were they so busy? When I asked about seating availability the greeter said it would be 20 minutes would I like to wait? That is not a long wait and I am sure I could entertain myself at the bar. As I looked around I found it was especially busy in special area referred to as the pizza bar. The Pizza bar was adjacent to the usual bar found in most restaurants. There was a great deal of energy surrounding this area.

My favorite activity is people watching so my interest was aroused. I made my way as close as possible to the pizza bar. It did not take long to understand the attraction. There was a slightly built, slender, black man, probably mid 30's making pizza. It wasn't what he was doing; it was how he performed his job. He was talking with the crowd of customers layers-deep at the pizza bar which flowed over to the beverage bar. He was constantly moving, at a brisk pace, while at the same time appeared effortless in his activities. While all the time he was explaining the ingredients in the pizza he was making. During his conversation with the audience he explained who the servers were at the restaurant that evening.

Michael understood how to make people feel special

Every so often he would call out to one of the servers by name, when one of their customer's pizza orders was ready for pick up. As the server approached to pick up their customers order, he would tell a complimentary story about the server. Next he was passing around a plate, with bite sizes pieces of a pizza he had just pulled out of the oven. The Pizza maker went on to explain the pizza which we are now tasting is his latest creation. This tasty delight was not something listed on the menu, but a special creation just for those customers at the bar tonight. After the plate of 2" square sample was empty the Pizza man began asking for feedback on his newest creation. This generated conversation among many of the people enjoying the complimentary treat. His treatment of customers made them each feel special. They had the opportunity to taste something not listed on the menu and then survey for feedback.

It was time for the Pizza man to announce another pizza order calling to the server whose table would receive the delivery. It was a different server than the previous order, so the Pizza man introduced this next server, as they approached the pizza bar for their order, followed by a complimentary story about the server. It was like having a pizza making cheerleader tossing out compliments to his co-workers.

If you make a stranger smile, you have made a friend.

He had a special knack of keeping people entertained, sometimes laughing, and always feeling they were going to receive special service regardless of which servers section they would be seated. After watching pizza man for a while it was easy to understand why he was so slender, he never stopped moving, or talking. This was a most pleasurable experience.

If you are not having fun; you are doing it wrong!

After finishing a great meal and paying my bill I asked to speak with the manager to find out more about the pizza man at the pizza bar. The pizza man's name is Michael. The manager went on to say, about 18 years earlier he observed Michael picking up litter in the parking lot of a restaurant he was managing at the time. After several day of this activity Michael approached the manager for a job. Michael did not possess any restaurant skills so the manager took a gamble and hired Michael to wash floors, clean the bathrooms, and other basic janitorial work. Michael was a hard worker always looking for things he could make better. The manager said from the beginning Michael was always respectful of co-workers. When the manager departed the original restaurant for another job he took Michael with him. The two had been working together for over 18 years. During that time Michael was always looking for new skills to learn. Even working full time as a pizza maker, Michael still comes to work when the restaurant is closed, to do handyman jobs. The manager said several times how Michael makes his job so much easier because he makes everyone around him a little better. Michael is not a manager, but his positive attitude helps his co-workers enjoy their job. Michael is always looking for ways that he can help people around him. The fun Michael is having is contagious. Such enthusiasm puts smiles on his co-workers faces. Their positive attitude is then passed on to the customers served. Next thing you know the entire restaurant is having fun.

Anything can be accomplished if no one worries about who gets credit

What do Fred and Michael have in common? They both understood Job One. Regardless of the job title or responsibility everyone has the same Job One. Make others glad they met you. Becoming a Job One success is not really hard.

So what is job one? I believe the foundation skill for every human being, is to make everyone you come into contact with, glad they met you. It is not possible to make every person you ever come in contact glad they met you, but if you never try, you will never accomplish one success.

It is hard when we try and fail; is worse to never have tried and succeed.

Job one, is having the ability to cause another person leave an experience with you thinking "I am glad I met that person today". What is most amazing is that it doesn't take much to stimulate such a reaction. Here are some of the ways we can make others glad they met us.

So what does it take to get that "I am glad I met that person", reaction?

- Knowledge

Michael was constantly learning new skills which continued to make him even more valuable to his boss. The knowledge Fred had allowed him to quickly evaluate a situation and understand who he could trust and who to avoid is the reason he was able to stay alive. Having the knowledge to help other people, makes a person more interesting, as well as, more sought after. Acquiring knowledge is an everyday pursuit. Constant learning increases a person value to others. Have you ever passed another person who appears lost? It could be in the airport, grocery store, mall, at work, but somewhere and you can see they look lost. How often does someone take the time to say "hey, do you need some help", or "can I help you" or "you look a bit puzzled, can I be of help". I see this every day and when I have offered assistance I am rewarded with another person's appreciation. Do I help everyone with this expression? Unfortunately, not. Too often I am self-absorbed with my daily activities of life. Schedules and time commitments often distract me from being more helpful, but I am trying to be better.

- Answer a Question

I have always taught customer service reps or sales people who work for me to answer customer's questions to help their situation, even if that means referring the customer to a competitor. When you solve another person problem or help them answer a question you are making their life easier. This will be remembered and rewarded with future requests. Throughout my life I have been amazed at the customer who sought me out because I help solve a problem with a competitor's product. The more knowledge a person possesses the more questions they can answer and the easier it is to make friends.

- Solve a Problem

Like answering questions in the best interest of others, solving problems make people glad they met you. This means answering questions with more than just a yes or no answer. It means finding the correct answer to a person's needs. The greatest accomplishment in any one's life is to become the go to person (factotum) for another human being. When you possess the knowledge and information to help others, there is no greater purpose in life.

When a person or company becomes the primary source for answers for another person or company they become an indispensable resource.

- Services

The smallest service or assistance such as comforting an ailing friend as Fred did for his pack members or Michael coming into work on his off hours to do maintenance around the restaurant. Each producing the "I am glad I met them response"

- Treat them to food

All creatures on earth get pleasure out of eating. Food is a basic need of life. Friendship can begin with a simple cup of coffee. When people share meals together they build personal bonds. As stated in earlier chapters food is a powerful motivator.

- Tell a story

We enjoy entertainment whether it is a stand-up comic telling funny stories making us laugh or a leader providing a learning moment story with a moral. Most people learn better when they can relate information to a story or an experience. Michael was an expert at entertaining his customers with stories of his co-workers. Fred built relationships because he gave customers an entertaining experience which they could share with family and friends.

- Compliment

Michael built customer loyalty because he was constantly complimenting his co-workers. Such compliments build confidence in co-workers. Confident people are more successful; compliments and confidence helps build team work. It is amazing the impact one person can have on another individual with a sincere compliment. Words can be very powerful such as "you were great" or WOW, "you did a terrific...." or "I am impressed". Remember, the giver of a compliment receives greater physiologic benefits via neurotransmitters than those receiving the compliment.

- Listening

The greatest form of flattery is to put your needs aside and listen to another person. If you want to make another person glad they met you, all you have to do is listen. Who is the most interesting person you know? Yourself! What topic do you spend the most time talking about? Yourself! You are the most interesting person you know and you love to talk about yourself. Because we find ourselves to be so interesting it is difficult to listen to another person. It is not natural to listen. When we take the time to listen it makes others feel good about them. Julie proved that to us and so did Fred.

- Thank you

When was the last time you sent a thank you note...maybe I should ask, have you ever sent a thank you note? Based on the response I get when I send such notes, I know it does not happen very often. These are very powerful. Especially when sent through an unusual method, via U.S. Postal Service. In today age of e-communications hand written thank you notes are rare, which is why they make a big impression on the recipient. I have visited offices where one of my hand written thank you notes on display in a customer's office and what is most amazing, it is years old. That note has served as a daily reminder for years. Verbal compliments are like compliments, also beneficial to the giver.

- Smile

The world's most powerful aphrodisiac, is a smile. Humans are drawn toward others who smile. Michael, while making pizzas and telling stories, he was always smiling or laughing. Fred's purse hunting and window display antics made people smile and caused people to want to meet him. When we smile we smell different because a smile stimulates the secretion of endorphins and serotonin which produce feelings of energy and happiness. Compared to when we frown, we do not enjoy the same neurotransmitter chemical feelings. Dogs instantly react different to a person smiling than when they are frowning, because the person smells different. Think about it.

Here is a pretty good way to live, whenever you are within 15 feet of another person smile, when you are within 5 feet of another person greet them.

Every day of my life, I continue to be amazed at the power of a simple smile.

People who smile live longer.

People who smile look younger

People who smile attract other people.

People who smile are fun to be with.

People who smile have lower blood pressure.

People who smile have high level of self-confidence.

People who smile have more energy.

People, who smile, are viewed by others as leaders.

People, who smile, are viewed by others as confident.

People, who smile, keep others wondering what they maybe thinking.

If you can't do anything else to make people glad they met you....at least smile, you will smell better.

JOB ONE = MAKING OTHERS GLAD THEY MET YOU

Be Aware of Your Thoughts
Because Your Thoughts Become
Your Words
Be Aware of Your Words
Because Your Words Become
Your Actions
Be Aware of Your Actions
Because Your Actions Become
Your Habits
Be Aware of Your Habits
Because Your Habits Become
Your Values
Be Aware of Your Values
Because Your Values Become
Your Destiny

Epilogue

Chapter 15

If you want to promote someone to a leadership position observe how they interact with animals. For example give an eight week old puppy to an employee you would like to promote into a leadership position. Follow up on the human-puppy relationship six months later and you will find what type of leader you have. If the puppy is cowering in fear you have an authoritarian leader, otherwise known as a bully. You will probably find the human yelling at the puppy and harshly reprimanding the puppy.

If the puppy is let to do as it pleases without any controls or directives you have a laisse-faire leader. You have found someone uninterested in training, leading, or learning, a non-leader.

If you find the human constantly trying to negotiate with the puppy to follow directions, or providing "if you" bribes. Puppy, if you sit than I will give you this reward. I see a lot of this behavior by parents trying to coax desired behavior out of their children.

None of these behaviors are examples of leadership. If, after six months you return to find a happy playful puppy with confidence, not fearful or scared, inquisitive, yet when the human makes a request of the puppy, such as come, sit, down, or other command, and the puppy makes an attempt to fulfill the request you have a leader. The puppy may not preform the desired task perfectly, but out of respect, trust, consistency, and confidence that may not be natural but instilled though time working together training, patiently communicating, and building honest feedback the puppy will try to react appropriately to the leader's request.

GLOSSARY

Artificial Pack (Organization): are groups made up of strangers, assembled into teams or work units to achieve a specific goal.

Avoidance Behavior: the act of refraining from doing something or preventing something from happening.

Corporate Culture: the values, customs, and traditions of a particular organization.

Extinguishment of Behavior: Is a fundamental concept of behavior psychology. It is a re-programing of learning to reduce or eliminate the frequency a specific behavior.

Finish Line Phenomenon: This is a common behavior of people attaining goals but not surpassing goals. Once they have achieved their goals they have a let-down in drive.

Firehouse Management: the behavior of management to constantly spend work hours putting out fires due to lack or planning, preparation or training.

Fixed Schedule Reinforcement: providing reinforcement, as a training tool, on a pre-planned schedule every time a desired behavior is displayed.

Formal Organization: Organizations have an organizational chart with specifically written job titles and descriptions which constitutes the formal organization.

Heel Position: This is a term used to describe an obedience foundation exercise, demonstrated by having both handler and dog facing the same direction with the dogs head in alignment with the handler's hip.

High Value Treats: rewards that are perceived, by the recipient, as very attractive, such that it motivates or rewards behavior.

Informal Organization: is how, in reality, without formal titles groups of people actually interact and function as a pack or an organization.

Ivan Pavlov: the father of classical conditioning, which connected a stimulus (bell) with reward (food) to shape behavior.

Learned Behavior or imprinting: is an automatic response to a stimulus that will repeat with consistency.

Learned Confidence: Those who are born without confidence can improve their confidence by employing such techniques as training, consistent behavior, goal setting, respect, and proofing as useful methods toward building confidence

Maslow's Hierarchy of Needs: created in 1943, it is a motivational theory in psychology comprising five tiers of needs, from primary needs such as shelter and food to the highest need of self-actualization.

Mushroom Management: The behavior of management to keep employees in the dark and feed the manure.

Natural Pack (Organization):   are the basic social structure in the human and animal world, a natural pack is most simply defined as a family unit.

Operant Conditioning: Is a fundamental concept of behavior psychology. It is a form of learning in which the strength of a behavior is modified by the behaviors consequence.

Posturing: is behavior that is exaggerated or affected, especially as an attempt to impress or deceive others.

Programing: establish a desired behavior in another by continuous and consistent reward or punishment.

Proofing: testing of a response or ability to respond properly to a stimulus when under a variety of challenging conditions.

Punishment: A penalty that is imposed for wrong doing.

Recognition: The acknowledgement of another's existence, their contribution, or act performed.

Redirect: change the interest of a subject by offering an alternative stimulus.

Reprimand: a formal rebuke or official reproof by a person in authority correcting subordinates.

Resource Guarding: An insecure dog can see anyone as a potential threat to a resource whether that resource is food, toys, space, a mate or access to a person.

Reward: Something positive that follows a desired response to a stimulus and acts to encourage desired behavior.

Seagull Management: the behavior of management to fly into a business unit deposit dropping all over its employees and fly away.

Social Learning Theory: Is a theory of learning the social behavior which proposes that new behavior can be acquired by observing and imitating others.

Superman complex: It is a behavior exhibited by a manager who believes they are the only person to rush into a situation.

Stimulus: Something that incites action, feeling, thought or exertion of effort by another.

Targeting: is the behavior of bullies focusing their attention on another individual they feel poses a threat or is weak and vulnerable.

Shaping Behavior: is a term, created by, Harvard Professor, B. F. Skinner, defining progressive changing of behavior by taking small steps toward an ultimate end. There are a wide variety of techniques as to how.

Variable Schedule Reinforcement: providing reinforcement, as a training tool, on a random schedule, when the desired behavior has been shown.

Reality:

It's estimated that in 2017 there were 89.7 million dogs (up from 68 million dogs in 2000) and 85.8 million cats are owned in the United States. Approximately 44% of all households in the United States have a dog, and 35% have a cat, for a total of 68% have a pet.

Dogs are euthanized each year:

It is hard to get a completely accurate answer, because not all shelters report, or are required to report, all euthanasia's. The HSUS estimates that animal shelters care for between 6-8 million dogs and cats every year in the United States, of whom approximately 3-4 million are euthanized. When factoring in the number of independent shelters and veterinarian clinics that also euthanize that number more realistically is 7-8 Million per year, or more. At this time The HSUS can only estimate these figures because there is no central data reporting agency for animal shelters. This overpopulation of companion animals is widely acknowledged across the country by professionals and experts in the animal welfare field. Overpopulation is a tragedy. There are simply not enough responsible homes for all of these wonderful, innocent animals. At this point in time, it would be impossible to humanely house every unwanted animal in the United States.

Dogs are running the streets of major cities:

A bigger problem is the number of stray dogs, which is estimated as high as 70 Million dogs. Houston alone estimates they have 1.2 million strays. The life expectancy of a stray dog on the streets is 3-4 months. To maintain this huge number of stray on our city street means the number of new strays is added every day.

Please

Neuter or spay

all Dogs, Cats,

and Humans

Russell Hornfisher has spent over 40 years working for companies in a variety of industries. He has held positions ranging from District Sales Manager to President. In his spare time, during the most recent 30 years, he fostered, trained, showed and judged dogs. Prior to getting involved with dogs, Russell earned a Master's of Science Degree in Organizational Behavior and Development. After his involvement with dogs, accompanied by one of his four legged teacher's assistants, he taught evening classes, on a variety of business topics at University of Northern Iowa and Eastern Michigan University as an adjunct instructor.

For over 20 years he has been a public speaker at conventions, business meetings, and business associations on topic such as:

How to Treat You Employees like a Dog
Who Moved My Dog Dish
Overheads and Golden Retrievers
In Dog Years
Selling Like a Dog
Pack Behavior
Don't Bark
Best in Show
Job One

His presentations deal with common skills used both in working with dogs and in building business organizations. Russell uses examples of dog training to demonstrate leadership skills necessary in growing successful businesses.

This book is the culmination of what he has learned over 20 years of presenting these programs.